BUM RAP ON AMERICA'S CITIES

THE REAL CAUSES OF URBAN DECAY

RICHARD S. MORRIS

PRENTICE-HALL, INC., Englewood Cliffs, N.J.

To Eileen McGann Hoats,
Jane Trichter, and
Alan Schwartz

Bum Rap on America's Cities: The Real Causes of Urban Decay, by Richard S. Morris

Printed in the United States of America

Prentice-Hall International, Inc., London
Prentice-Hall of Australia, Pty. Ltd., Sydney
Prentice-Hall of Canada, Ltd., Toronto
Prentice-Hall of India Private Ltd., New Delhi
Prentice-Hall of Japan, Inc., Tokyo
Prentice-Hall of Southeast Asia Pte. Ltd., Singapore
Whitehall Books Limited, Wellington, New Zealand

10 9 8 7 6 5 4 3 2 1

Library of Congress Cataloging in Publication Data

Morris, Richard S
Bum rap on America's cities.

Includes bibliographical references and index.
1. Cities and towns—United States. I. Title.
HT123.M65 301.36'3'0973 77-17196
ISBN 0-13-089227-0

CONTENTS

Acknowledgements *vi*

Introduction *1*

1 Get the Middle Class Off Welfare *15*

2 The Medicaid Mess *33*

3 The Bank Strike *51*

4 Who Creates Slums? *67*

5 The Energy Windfall *85*

6 The Supermarket Swindle *99*

7 How the Northeast Loses Its Money *109*

8 The Discriminatory Federal Income Tax *119*

9 No Federal Jobs for the Northeast *141*

10 The Pentagon:
A Five-sided Building That Faces South *147*

11 How Washington Pays
the Northeast in Confederate Money *153*

12 How the Northeast
Gets Cheated by Federal Aid Programs *175*

A Final Thought *185*

Notes *189*

Index *195*

Acknowledgements

I am most of all indebted to Dr. Alan Schwartz of Queens Borough Community College for his assistance and guidance in the preparation of this book. His advice and wisdom were of immense help in translating idea into text and text into argument.

Michael O'Keefe was also indispensable, spending endless hours digging up data and pouring through obscure public documents. His hours, combined with his skill, made this book possible.

Robert Stewart of Prentice-Hall has been much more than an editor to me, but rather a guide, an inspiration, and a constructive critic. I shall be indebted to him for his assistance for a very long time.

I want particularly to thank two people whose inspiration were pivotal to my work and whose initial and constant encouragement made it possible: City Councilwoman Jane Trichter and Paul D. Feinstein.

Elizabeth Hauser deserves my special thanks and appreciation for her role in making this book possible.

Finally, my wife, Eileen McGann Hoats, herself an expert on a host of issues raised in this work, was a constant source of encouragement, wisdom, guidance, and love, as always.

INTRODUCTION

The four volumes of tissue-thin paper were piled high on the corner of my desk. Their single-spaced, cramped listing of names and addresses was a strain to the eye; the list seemed endless. I had anticipated, when I first ordered a computer printout of the names of those who had lost their jobs in the New York City budget crisis, that the listing would span a few hundred pages of small print. I ordered it to complete a study for the Community Service Society, a New York social welfare organization, of the geographic distribution of layoffs during the recent fiscal nightmare that had gripped New York. I was totally unprepared for the four thousand pages of small type, costing over two thousand dollars just to print on a computer.

The list read like the casualty rolls in the sixties from Vietnam or the lists of the dead after an air disaster. Each name denoted a separate loss of dignity, interruption of income, and termination of a dream of security, comfort, and fulfillment. The names were like a roll call of the victims.

Like the casualties of a war, the loss of city jobs had struck close to home. My former wife had been fired from her job in the city high schools, a close friend laid off as an investigator at the Department of Consumer Affairs, and another let go by the City Hospital Corporation. At every party, in every gathering, it seemed that somebody had just lost his job and had been forced to search for sustenance in a job market so forbidding that it had left New York State with the second highest unemployment rate in the nation. But the 50,000 fired city workers were nothing compared to the 700,000 jobs that had left New York since 1969 and the massive unemployment that gripped the states of the Northeast from Massachusetts to Illinois.

One can imagine the final day at work for city employees who receive their dreaded pink slips announcing that their services are no longer required. As these innocent victims of the urban crisis pack their briefcases and clean out their desks in the municipal office building on Chambers Street in lower Manhattan, they might walk over to the windows of that magnificent old structure and gaze for the last time upon the incomparable view of the downtown New York skyline. Their gaze might first drift to the towering buildings of Wall Street and the financial district, once reminders of the depth of New York's economic power, now grim monuments to the 35,000 securities jobs lost in New York since 1969. Beyond their imposing facades lie the rotting piers and abandoned wharves that comprise the once proud, thriving, and bustling Port of New York. Out in the water stands the glorious Statue of Liberty, holding aloft her torch and proclaiming her message of relief to the "tired" and "poor" of the world, those "huddled masses yearning to breathe free." Her message must indeed seem bankrupt to the city workers who shuffle out of their offices each day into a job market with an unemployment rate about 50 percent higher than the national average.

Indeed, once America's cities were her economic core. To their streets came millions of Americans in search of jobs, cultural opportunities, and a new life as well as tens of millions of immigrants from impoverished foreign shores. As recently as 1968, New York, Boston, and dozens of other cities had unemployment rates below the national average. Now almost every northeastern city experiences joblessness well above the national norm, some as much as 70 percent higher. From Newark to Minneapolis and Buffalo to Milwaukee, the cities of the Northeast were in desperate trouble. Unemployment was only one of their problems. Increasingly, inflation had devastated them far more than it had affected the rest of America. The same energy that costs $15 in Houston, one of the new cities of the Sun Belt, costs $37 in New York and $25 in Philadelphia and Boston. It costs $27,000 to live in New York or Boston at a life-style that costs only $18,500 in a rural southern town.

It is no wonder that they looked forward so desperately to the onset of the Carter administration for relief. Indeed, just forty-eight hours after the polls closed in 1976, the mayors of America's cities gathered in Chicago in emergency session to ask the new President-elect for assistance and aid. Mayor Kenneth A. Gibson of Newark sounded the theme when he asked that Carter "set a national tone of concern for urban America." The Ford-Nixon years had not been good for American cities. Housing subsidies were impounded, water pollution control aid halted, the school lunch program truncated, hospital construction curtailed, vocational education assistance leveled off, and a host of federal subsidies reduced. Indeed, federal aid to New York City, which had risen by 80 percent a year under Johnson, now rose by barely 11 percent annually under Nixon and Ford—scarcely enough to keep pace with inflation. Indeed, in the midst of the New York fiscal crises, Washington cut its aid to New York by $200 million. The New York *Daily News* said it all on October 30, 1975, when its headline blared, "Ford to

City: Drop Dead," as the President rejected New York's entreaty for some federal assistance in its financial predicament.

Cities could not have taken much more punishment and, like a punch-drunk fighter, they staggered glassy-eyed into the final months of 1976 hoping for a new national administration, for an end to the battering and punishment that had been their lot for eight years. But the Nixon-Ford barrage had more than an economic impact. It was felt in more than a cutoff in aid or a reduction in federal urban programs. The national administration had launched a successful campaign to break the spirit of urban liberalism. Just as a fighter loses his self-confidence long before he sees stars at the end of a bout, America's northeastern cities have been stripped of their belief in their ideology.

The conservative theme was simple. It originated in what Dan Rather and Gary Paul Gates called the "Social Issue" to explain the decay of the northeastern city. The "Social Issue" was first developed, they explain in their book *The Palace Guard,* by Nixon and Agnew for use in the 1970 national congressional elections. As they describe it, "The President instructed Agnew to hammer away at the permissiveness theme without letup. The Democrats, he said, must be blamed for everything from campus protest to drugs to pornography to the whole general breakdown of law and order—in other words, the gamut of what came to be known that year as the Social Issue." Increasingly, conservatives tied this social theme to the deterioration of cities. Permissiveness had led to a wave of moral deterioration that was carrying cities to their doom. High taxes, proconsumer laws, labor unions, environmental sensitivities, and the social laws of the northeastern city were proving lethal and making it impossible for the nation's older urban areas to compete with the Sun Belt.

Welfare cheats and those who advocated major social spending occupied key places in the litany of conservative villains. Perhaps the most lucid articulation of this conservative ideology came from former Senator James L. Buckley in his reply in *The New York Times* Op-Ed page to Senator

Daniel Patrick Moynihan, who defeated him in their 1976 battle for the New York Senate seat. Moynihan had spoken out saying that "I have reached the conclusion that our decline [as a city] has come about as the direct and palpable consequence of the policies of the Federal Government." Moynihan's theses were attacked by Buckley, who noted:

- It wasn't Washington that dictated the level of welfare benefits (30 percent higher than the six next most generous states) that drew so many of the nation's poor to New York in the 1950s and 60s.
- It wasn't Washington that induced New York City to retain rent control laws that have led to the abandonment of hundreds of thousands of housing units and the savaging of the city's tax base.
- It wasn't Washington that caused New York to gold-plate its services, or pioneer moral-obligation debt financing, or run up state and local taxes to levels 50 percent higher than those obtaining in the neighboring industrial states with which New York must compete.
- It wasn't Washington that mandated municipal employee pension fringe benefits so far in excess of the national average that they add more than an additional billion dollars to New York City's budget.
- It wasn't the explosion of Federal spending in the late 1960s that caused New York City to lose one out of six manufacturing jobs in the period from 1950 through 1964.

According to the conservatives, it wasn't Washington's fault; it was the permissiveness and liberal social generosity of the urban Northeast that brought about its economic decay. On the strength of the campaign against permissiveness, Frank Rizzo in Philadelphia, Louise Day Hicks in Boston, and Mario Procaccino in New York built their careers and carved out their political base. City politics throughout America assumed the aspect of a perpetual clash between the John Lindsays and Carl Stokeses and Kevin Whites—the bearers of the New Deal tradition—and their conservative critics. Archie and Edith Bunker squared off against Franklin and Eleanor Roosevelt in a battle for the soul of America's cities.

Like most New Yorkers, I found myself increasingly drawn into this battle, impelled by a fear that a Frank Rizzo could become mayor of New York City or governor of New York State and determined to continue the urban impetus toward social democracy. After I left Columbia in 1967, I went to work for the Citizens Budget Commission, a business-oriented civic watchdog group charged with overseeing municipal finances in New York and accustomed to regular criticism of excessive spending and borrowing. My six years there gave me a deep familiarity with all aspects of city finance and a fundamental belief that urban liberalism could succeed if only it were properly managed and intelligently run. Increasingly, I began to work with liberal Democratic political leaders and candidates in New York taking advantage of my familiarity with city finance to gain access to them and to help shape their ideas. I tried to point out that the problems New York was facing were a consequence of national policies on the one hand and local mismanagement on the other, but not the result of any error in direction or approach. It was clear to me that permissivism had as little to do with the urban malaise as it had to do with national economic problems. It was a smoke screen set off by those who have historically sought to undermine liberal policies but who have despaired of direct attacks.

By 1974 I began to work with political candidates and officials through my own consulting firm, the Public Affairs Research Organization. I wrote hundreds of speeches, press statements, and issue papers for an array of New York City political leaders including 1974 gubernatorial candidate Howard J. Samuels, City Comptroller Harrison J. Goldin, City Council President Paul O'Dwyer, Manhattan Borough President Percy E. Sutton, Bronx Borough President Robert Abrams, and New York State Assembly Speaker Stanley Steingut. In 1975 I expanded my work to a national level and began working with candidates and legislators throughout the nation. My clients included three current United States senators, a dozen members of Congress, and governors or lieutenant governors in Vermont, Ohio, Massachusetts, and Minnesota.

My work took me into a variety of states including Vermont, Massachusetts, Rhode Island, New Jersey, Pennsylvania, Virginia, North Carolina, Kansas, Nebraska, Wisconsin, Minnesota, Ohio, Indiana, Iowa, and Colorado. In each state, I broadened my perspective and began to understand more fully the national patterns at work in the decline of America's cities. As I worked in the other states of the Northeast, I saw that the problems with which I was accustomed to dealing in New York were not unique to my native city, but endemic to a band of urban areas running from Boston through New York and Philadelphia, and out through Cleveland to Chicago and Minneapolis.

Inevitably, my clients—who were exclusively liberal Democrats—were facing challenges from the Rizzo-Hicks-Archie Bunker factions in their own states and cities, and I was called upon to fashion replies and write answers to these attacks. Almost every day, I seemed to be drafting a speech or a statement defending urban liberalism against an onslaught charging that permissivism was at the core of urban decay. I began to become extremely wary of conservative tirades about liberal urban permissivism. It seemed increasingly that behind their ardent desire to trim certain programs and expand others, there lay a quotient of greed which was hard to ignore.

By 1975 the conflict that had been brewing since the late sixties between urban liberals and conservatives exploded into a raging national debate, triggered by the near default of New York City and the evident trouble in its economy. The urban economic crisis had been aggravated by the national depression of 1974-75 to the point where it was no longer a regional or local issue, but the center of national focus. In the conservative view, decades of permissivism toward welfare recipients, labor unions, municipal employees, minority groups, and environmentalists had finally come home to roost. They received news of New York's disastrously unbalanced budget and looming economic collapse with an I-told-you-so attitude that gave them the decisive upper hand in the formulation of municipal fiscal and economic policy.

There could be no more speculation about the true gravity of the urban crisis. New York City was virtually bankrupt and other cities were teetering on the brink. Business had begun to leave the cities in massive numbers. New York City alone lost over 700,000 jobs—about a fifth of its total—between 1969 and 1977. Every day newspapers were filled with reports of major corporations relocating out of America's cities, moving South or to suburban communities.

No longer were only right-wing political leaders like Buckley, Rizzo, Hicks, and Procaccino attacking the liberal drift of America's urban governments. Instead, political leaders squarely in the mainstream joined the attack. The most articulate of these converts to the political right was New York State's commerce commissioner, John Dyson, who laid out the conservative political agenda in a February 2, 1976, *New York Times* article headlined "State's Commerce Chief Asks Fiscal Shift to Right."

The *Times* noted that "a strategy for rebuilding the sagging economy of the state that would turn government policy sharply to the right and give first priority to the needs of business is being put together by Governor Carey's new commerce commissioner, John S. Dyson." The Dyson program included:

- Lowering the tax rate on the highest incomes to keep businessmen from moving themselves and their companies to states with no income tax.
- Phasing out many regulations on business.
- Imposing a temporary moratorium on the requirement that environmental impact statements be filed for all public projects.
- Extending to the whole of the state the business tax credits for expanding manufacturing plants.
- Stopping efforts to restructure utility rates that would force higher costs on large industrial users.

In explaining his position as a member of a liberal Democratic administration advocating a shift to the right, Dyson said that it was possible for a liberal Democrat like Governor Carey to propose and get enacted a tax reduction for the rich just as a Republican like former President Richard M. Nixon was able to soften the nation's hard line on Communist China and establish diplomatic relations with that country.

The Dyson message brought quick results in New York. Governor Carey warned, in his 1975 State of the State message, that "the days of wine and roses are over." Carey demonstrated the change in the attitude of the state government when he broke publicly with his environmental conservation commissioner, Ogden Reid, who sought to curb General Electric's plants at Fort Edward and Hudson Falls, New York, alleging that they were pumping PCBs (polychlorinated biphenyls), a carcinogen, into the Hudson River, polluting drinking and fishing waters. Reid had dealt harshly with General Electric, insisting that they desist from the dumping and pay a heavy fine for having polluted the Hudson. Carey publicly proclaimed the importance of tempering environmental concerns with economic realism and removed Reid as commissioner, presumably to clear the way for a more moderate settlement with General Electric.

The most concrete manifestation of the new wave of conservative austerity came, of course, in New York City where over 50,000 city workers lost their jobs, social programs were reduced, tuition imposed at the historically free City University, services reduced at the city hospitals, and tax incentives for business hastily enacted. It seemed that liberals were perpetually on the defensive and progressivism could no longer find a safe haven in city halls or northeastern state houses.

The discomfort of liberals was brought home to me most clearly during a luncheon with New York Assemblyman Oliver Koppell, one of the most liberal members of the State Assembly, who had played a leading role in the 1975 legislative session in demanding greater public regulation of banks to promote investment in poor neighborhoods, now largely refused loans and mortgages by cautious savings bankers. Koppell would not exactly have been welcomed at a bankers' convention or a gathering of the Chamber of Commerce. Now we were meeting to discuss what Koppell would focus on during the coming year. I had come to him with a set of proposals for new bank taxes to promote inner-city investment, state regulation to prohibit the denial of mortgage money to people based on the neighborhood in which they lived, and the creation of a state fund to lend where banks wouldn't. I frankly expected Koppell to embrace the proposals as quickly as I could articulate them.

I wasn't prepared for the reaction I got. He moved his six-foot-three-inch frame forward, leaned over his lunch, and asked me earnestly, "But don't we have to worry about what these ideas will do to the business climate?" I couldn't believe that this was the single most liberal member of the legislature talking. "Don't we have to be concerned that all these taxes and regulations will so alienate business that they will just leave?" I explained that banks couldn't very well leave, that their depositors were here and that they couldn't just move away. But Koppell persisted, "I don't mean that the banks will leave, but won't all this create a bad climate for other businesses?" I didn't know if Koppell had been transformed or if I was in the wrong place.

I've had a lot of conversations like that in the past few years. Koppell isn't alone in doubting whether his liberal views are really appropriate to our economic problems. Many hardened liberals are beginning to wonder if the New Deal and the Great Society have not left us with a legacy of spending and deficits from which cities can never recover. They ask if the trend toward government regulation and oversight has not just left a pile of paperwork and hampered economic growth. Former supporters of Ralph Nader and once ready participants in Earth Day and ecology demonstrations are beginning to have doubts—have they gone too far?

But, by 1975 and 1976, a backlash had begun to set in. Liberals had witnessed how facile and empty the Nixon rhetoric about permissivism had been as they watched

Watergate engulf those who had been calling for law and order. Exposés about huge larceny in the nursing home and Medicaid programs and stories that began to appear in *The Village Voice* about real estate and banking profits stemming from the New York City fiscal crisis whetted the curiosity of urban liberals about whether the conservative rhetoric packaged for home consumption in the American city was just as cynically self-serving and misleading. A suspicion began to grow and fester that perhaps liberals were taking a bum rap and were not responsible for all the ills of the American city. Perhaps there were forces at work behind the scenes driving New York to decay and bankruptcy and undermining every northeastern city quite apart from the welfare cheats and overspenders whom conservatives attacked and blamed. Kirkpatrick Sale added to the momentum when his work *The Power Shift* argued that the Northeast was losing out to the Sun Belt in the battle for regional supremacy. A series in *The New York Times* and other publications began to sound the same theme.

I was caught up in this backlash. My clients began to ask for material that demonstrated that the Nixon-Ford view about the causes of the urban crises were inaccurate. New York Assembly Speaker Stanley Steingut asked me to examine how the refusal of banks to lend money in urban areas was causing housing decay. Manhattan Borough President Percy E. Sutton wanted data showing how much welfare money never went to the poor for whom it was intended, but ended up instead in the pockets of doctors, landlords, and city employees. Vermont Governor Thomas P. Salmon asked me to develop papers on how the federal government shortchanged the Northeast by not giving it a fair share of national spending. Ohio Senator Howard Metzenbaum wanted data showing that the energy crisis had unfairly hurt the Northeast and profited the oil companies. Essentially, each was asking for the same thing: proof that it was not liberalism that was to blame for the Northeast's economic disaster. They wanted to be able to answer those who said "we told you so"—that liberal regulatory and spending policies would lead to ruin.

This book argues that liberals are, indeed, taking a bum rap in shouldering the blame for the fiscal and economic decay of the American city. In attacking permissivism, labor unions, consumerism, social welfare, environmental concerns, and other favorite targets of the right, we miss the point. The cities are being punished by a very different cast of villains and are suffering at their hands far more profoundly and far more permanently:

- *The Welfare Profiteers:* Eighty percent of all money spent on welfare in New York City in 1976 did not go to poor people but went instead to middle-class providers of service, many of whom overcharged for providing the poor with medical care, nursing homes, housing, and social services. They are the true welfare cheats, and it is to reducing the cost of their services that we must look to contain the social welfare budget.
- *The Banks.* Right-wing mythology argues that the banks decided to withdraw from lending to American cities in 1975, recoiling in horror at the imbalance of the New York City budget and determined to protect their depositors from loss. The facts indicate that the banks withdrew from the cities in *1973,* well before there was any basis for concluding that cities were in trouble. The data indicates that banks more precipitated the urban fiscal crisis by driving up debt service costs than reacted to it once it was in full swing.
- *Mortgage Lenders.* Urban real estate is in desperate trouble not because of rent control laws—most cities don't even have them—but because of redlining, the refusal of mortgage lenders to invest in inner-city neighborhoods. Behind redlining lies the federal government. In 1975 Washington channeled 29 percent of its loan insurance to three states—Florida, California, and Arizona—which had, together, 15 percent of the country's population. By insuring loans in the Sun Belt and not in the Northeast, Washington led the way for the bank redlining of American cities.
- *The Income Tax System.* So prejudicial are the deductions and exemptions afforded in the federal tax

law to urban taxpayers that the citizens of New York City paid 6.8 percent of all federal income tax collections while they comprised only 3.6 percent of the national population. Renters cannot deduct property taxes and mortgage interest payments; homeowners can. Gasoline taxes are deductible, but urban energy-use taxes are not.

- *The Pentagon.* The federal defense budget is a subsidy to the South. With only 38 percent of the nation's population, the Sun Belt states get 50 percent of the defense budget. But the states of the Northeast, with 45 percent of the people, must be content with only 28 percent of the defense budget. These allocations drain wealth away from the Northeast and encourage the Sun Belt boom.
- *The Social Security System.* By failing to adjust its benefits for the radical differences in the regional cost of living in the North and in the Sun Belt which have arisen in recent years, federal programs such as Social Security, veterans' benefits, and food stamps pay more to the South, in real dollars, than they do to the North.
- *Energy Policy.* The Northeast faces a dire energy crisis. The rest of America has realized an energy bonanza as their cost of power has dropped far below that of the Northeast, bringing jobs, migrants, and corporations to the South in search of cheaper gas and oil.

Together, these problems saddle the Northeast with an insufferable economic and fiscal burden. They militate for a higher cost of living in the Northeast, higher taxes, fewer jobs, less income, and fewer government services. The fifteen states of the Northeast send to Washington $44 billion more in taxes than they get back in spending. The fifteen states of the Sun Belt get back from Washington $36 billion more in *spending* than they pay in *taxes.* Such a gap between the regions is the true cause of the urban fiscal and economic crisis. It is the true area in which we must make progress if we are to allow our cities to survive and recover. It is time to stop embracing slogans about welfare cheats and liberal excesses that have no meaning. We must rivet our attention on the real enemies of our cities and move ahead from there.

I.

GET THE MIDDLE CLASS OFF WELFARE

As the president of the Borough of Manhattan and one of the nation's leading elected black political leaders, I had assumed that Percy E. Sutton knew all there was to know about the problems of welfare. I was surprised when he called me and asked for a briefing on welfare issues as part of a presentation I was preparing for him on New York problems and issues. During his twelve years on the Board of Estimate, New York's chief legislative body, and through his unofficial status as the political leader of Harlem, he had fielded thousands of questions on welfare and debated it hundreds of times.

Nevertheless, he was shocked with the welfare data I

showed him. He, like almost every other political leader, had assumed that most of the welfare program spending went for aid to the poor. When I explained that over eighty cents of each welfare dollar spent in New York went to people who were not poor[1]—administrators, bureaucrats, doctors, hospitals, social workers, and others who provide services to the poor—Sutton was astounded. "I had no idea it was that high," Sutton said. "In other words, the welfare program is really only partially one for poor people; it is primarily a system of buying services from the middle class to be provided to the poor."

Since that briefing in 1976, I have heard Sutton hammer away at the theme that it is not the poor themselves who get most of the welfare money, but the middle-class providers of services to the poor. It is what we have to pay these providers of service, not what we pay the poor in their weekly checks, that causes welfare budgets to skyrocket. But despite Sutton and others, the myth remains set in the public's mind that it is welfare recipients who are breaking the back of the city treasury. From cabdriver to senator, it seems that everybody blames the problems of our cities on welfare spending. In New York City alone, health, welfare, and social services costs have risen from $400 million in 1960 to $4 billion today. One in every eight New Yorkers is on the welfare rolls. About one in four children is on welfare, and welfare and Medicaid absorb a third of the city's budget.[2] Nothing has come to symbolize more clearly to many the way liberal social policies have contributed to urban fiscal problems than the skyrocketing welfare budget.

The popular conception that welfare is a program primarily of cash grants to the poor springs, justifiably enough, from the historic fact that cash payments dominated the welfare program when it was originally conceived during the Roosevelt administration. When the Social Security Act of 1935 established a program of federal grants to states to assist them in relief of the destitute, blind, and of homeless, crippled, dependent, and delinquent children, welfare was little more than a cash handout.[3] No social services were provided as part of the program except for minimal support of public health programs. Welfare continued as a primarily cash grant program until the Great Society days of Lyndon Johnson.

Dismayed by the seeming inability of welfare recipients to lift themselves out of poverty, the Johnson administration embarked on a massive program of social legislation designed to augment the basic cash grant approach of welfare. Merely passing out money to the poor, it was argued, did not meet their social needs. Welfare mothers could not afford to find day care for their children, medical expenses were well beyond the reach of the average welfare family, job training and remedial education were not encompassed in the pre-Johnson welfare program. It was argued that all welfare cash grants could do was to give the recipient enough money to survive, but not to move up and become independent.

A spate of legislation followed during the Johnson years creating a host of social programs to provide day care, job training, medical services, remedial education, vocational education, and the like to the poor. The most expensive of these efforts was the Medicaid program, designed to make medical care easily available to the poor for the first time.

Together, these programs changed dramatically the nature of welfare. No longer a simple transfer of cash from government to poor people, the program now placed increasing emphasis on providing *services* to the poor as well as money. More and more funds went to those who provided these services (vendors of service in the language of most statutes), and these allocations absorbed an increasing share of the welfare dollar.

The focus of welfare spending shifted even more sharply to these vendors of service and away from cash payments to the poor as the impact of inflation became more severe in the early 1970s. Vendors of service were generally permitted to increase their charges for service to keep pace with high costs of living, welfare agency employees got salary raises, and medical service costs increased even more rapidly than was warranted by the general national rate of inflation.

While some social service vendors had to suffer under intermittent wage freezes and pressures to hold down spending, most found that they could pass along their increased costs to the public sector and expect reimbursement. But welfare recipients themselves had no such luck. In the face of virulent national inflation, state legislatures generally refused to permit increases in welfare cash grants. Indeed, under Governor Nelson Rockefeller, New York cut its welfare payment levels in 1971. Impelled by a popular backlash against welfare spending, political leaders fought to contain cash grant levels even though the living costs of the poor were rising rapidly. Thus, between 1972 and 1974, cash grants to welfare recipients, nationally, decreased by 5.2 percent while spending for medical care for the welfare poor rose 37 percent and spending on social services for the poor rose 43 percent.[4] Vendors of medical and social services, through their lobbyists, were able to insure that their increased costs were matched by increased public subsidy while the welfare recipient was forced to survive with less and less cash each year.

By now, welfare is thoroughly converted to a program whose main emphasis is on payments for *services* rather than payments for cash grants. In 1974, $25 billion was spent by local and state governments on public welfare. Ten billion was spent on cash payments to the poor—only 40 percent. The remainder went to those who provide the poor with services.

PUBLIC WELFARE COSTS OF STATE AND LOCAL GOVERNMENTS, 1972-74[5]

(in millions)

Type of Service	*1972*	*1973*	*1974*	*% Change*
Cash payments to the poor	$10.5	$11.1	$10.0	– 5.3
Purchase of medical care for the poor	6.1	7.1	8.4	+37.1
Purchase of social services for the poor	4.7	5.6	6.7	+42.7
TOTAL	$21.3	$23.8	$25.1	+17.6

But despite this dramatic shift from a program of cash payments to one of purchase of services, welfare has remained fixed in the public mind as a program of direct aid to poor people. Few realize how thoroughly it is a program of payments to the middle class to provide services such as housing, day care, foster care, job training, medical care, dental care, and others to the poor, nor how top-heavy with administrative staff welfare programs have become.

These providers of service are reimbursed by local government for the cost of the services they offer the poor. Local government is, in turn, reimbursed by state and federal funds for most of its outlay. Washington generally contributes 50 percent of the bill while states, cities, and counties divide the other half. In certain programs, such as Medicaid, the federal contribution is higher and in others it is lower. In each program, however, the key question is what the services provided the poor (medical, social, or housing) should cost and whether the services are necessary in the first place. These are both highly subjective decisions. It is relatively easy for a state legislature to vote to pay poor people $250 or $300 a month as a welfare grant, but the proper cost of services provided the poor is a more subtle issue. Because of the pressure by the real estate interests for more liberal allowances for welfare rent levels, by medical interests for generous Medicaid reimbursement fees, and by social service agencies for high day-care or foster-care payment levels, the proper cost of services delivered the poor is also the subject of some intense lobbying.

A corollary problem has been the rapid growth in the administrative overhead of the welfare program. New York City's Department of Social Services, for example, employs twenty thousand people, about as many as the New York City Police Department and more than the Fire and Sanitation departments combined. This enormous overhead costs $330 million in salary and fringe benefits alone. When one considers that New York pays its welfare recipients about $800 million, exclusive of reimbursement for their rent, it is ironic that New York City spends $1 to administer every $2 of welfare funding.[6]

It is in these two realms—the proper cost of services

provided the poor and the optimum level of administrative overhead—that the cost of welfare is primarily determined. The bulk of unnecessary welfare spending is generated through excessive charges for services provided the poor and abnormally high overhead costs. That object of universal scorn, the welfare cheat, is responsible for only a minor share of excessive welfare spending. The welfare mother who pretends her husband has left her so she can gain extra welfare benefits must take a back seat to the landlord who bills for excessive rents when he houses welfare families or the doctor who charges too much for his services treating Medicaid patients or the welfare administrator who adds to his staff at every opportunity increasing their cost to the taxpayer. In my view, these are the real welfare cheats, and it is only through close examination of their activity and more effective regulation of their practices that we will ever control the high cost of welfare and Medicaid in the American city.

I had a unique opportunity to understand the full magnitude of these overcharges for social services provided the poor when I was retained, in 1977, by a coalition of New York civic groups—Joint Action for Children—to study how money was being spent to provide foster care for children. Foster care is necessitated when a child is abandoned, abused, or neglected by its natural parents and must be placed in a foster home. Some children are located in private homes, where the parents are paid for taking the children, and others, generally the older and more disruptive children, are placed in a variety of small and large institutions and group homes for care.

Most foster care is provided through voluntary agencies rather than government departments, since these agencies—many religiously based—have historically offered the service. But while these agencies had done so in the past as an act of philanthropy, they now look to government to reimburse them for the "costs" of providing foster care. The agencies that provide foster care include some of the most politically powerful in New York City, including the leading Catholic, Jewish, and Protestant organizations.[7] It is an unwise politician who antagonizes these potent organizations, and, as a result, these agencies have been able to survive even the most recent round of budget cuts in New York City with their programs relatively intact (not larger, but not any smaller either).[8]

In theory, these agencies are reimbursed only for their actual costs of service. But, as I reviewed their budgets, I was astonished at what they were able to submit as "costs" of care. Public relations, financial, and legal departments were labeled as integral to the "costs" of care, and the overall cost of foster care exceeded nine thousand dollars per year per child. With 29,000 children in foster care, the bill to the city was staggering. Obviously, some of these costs were genuine, and many children were provided with excellent foster care, but my analysis indicated that spending on administration and overhead exceeded spending on direct services for children by a goodly margin. I found foster-care agencies that were spending over four thousand dollars per child just on overhead and administration.[9]

I asked Carol Parry, the director of the foster-care program, about these high costs. "Some are legitimate, but a lot are very high and amount to subsidies to some of these social agencies." I asked why these subsidies have not been cut more sharply, and Parry replied, "Haven't you seen who some of these agencies are? They are among the most powerful in New York City. I have been trying to keep their costs in line for years now, but they have a lot of influence and it isn't always easy and I'm not always successful."[10] Indeed, Parry pointed out that the budgets for these foster-care agencies did not even fall under her control but were lodged in the politically protected "Charitable Institutions Budget," an enclave in the New York City budget for payments to voluntary or philanthropic organizations.

High overhead costs like these have been built into many major social programs at their inception. Typically, programs like Medicaid, day care, drug-abuse treatment, and others were launched in response to a perceived urgent social need. Upon their initiation, enthusiastic legislative bodies would vote substantial sums of money to "lick the problem" well before there was developed any substantial capacity to spend the funds wisely. For example, the New York State Legislature, in 1970, became alarmed at the growing amount of drug addiction among teen-agers and the lack of successful efforts to cope with the problem. The Youthful Drug Abusers Program was passed in that year appropriating $65 million for drug-addiction treatment and prevention programs throughout the state. The money was dumped in the laps of local agencies who were told to go out and find drug-treatment programs to fund with the money. But few drug programs existed, and even these could not hope to expand quickly enough to use effectively all the money the state had voted. Yet local program administrators did not want to be caught at the end of the year with unspent money in their budgets and thus lay themselves open to the accusation that they did not do all they could to battle drug addiction. As a result, many fly-by-night groups were funded to provide what passed for drug treatment. One agency, funded under the program, was found to be paying for a large farm upstate which was providing an occasional refuge of dubious value to some potential young addicts, but was certainly furnishing a home of very great value to its owners, who were soon dropped from the program.[11]

Says Mitchell Rosenthal, the director of Phoenix House, the foremost of American drug-addiction treatment organizations, "There was a sudden flood of money for drug treatment in the late sixties and many of the groups which had been funded to do antipoverty work just turned around and hung up a new shingle outside offering 'encounter groups' and other nominal forms of addiction treatment to try to get drug money. It took many years to shake out the program and prune it down only to those groups and agencies rendering useful and legitimate therapy and to exclude those whose efforts were of more questionable value."[12]

In a sense, the War on Poverty, suddenly declared by President Johnson and vigorously pressed in the mid-sixties, had its own "war profiteers"—men and women attracted to the program by the prospect of easy funding and determined to take the government for as much as they could. Their efforts were abetted by the inexperience of many government program administrators and the simple absence of enough qualified applicants for antipoverty money to compete with the profiteers.

But in certain areas profiteering remained built into the program. In many areas of social legislation the "shakeout" to which Rosenthal refers in drug-addiction treatment simply did not take place. The profiteering remained embedded in the program and grew to new proportions. It is these excess charges that drive up urban welfare costs beyond all reason, not the legitimate demands for care and treatment of the poor, and certainly not the needs of the poor for weekly welfare money.

In this chapter, we will look briefly at three manifestations of this profiteering–real estate rentals, services to children, and administrative costs. In the next chapter, we will discuss Medicaid spending, which has led to its own pattern of excessive expenditure and overcharges for services.

HOUSING WELFARE RECIPIENTS

In 1974 I was hired by the New York University Real Estate Institute to study how to save two New York neighborhoods –Crown Heights and Washington Heights–from housing deterioration. Each community had witnessed a rapid erosion of its housing stock and seemed to be going the way of many other New York neighborhoods, slippage into deterioration and eventual total abandonment. The purpose of the study was to isolate the causes of the decay and to recommend ways of arresting it before it was too late. As part of the study, I examined data provided by Pratt Institute listing the incomes of Crown Heights tenants and the rents they paid. The Pratt data was printed out by a computer and listed the rent of each apartment and the income of the tenant occupying it. I examined the data in my office and found that in almost every case, tenants with "PA" next to their apartments were paying higher rents than were other tenants. I asked what "PA" meant and learned that it stood for "public assistance"—welfare.

In New York, as in almost every other city, welfare recipients receive an allowance for rent that equals the full amount due unless the rent is above a ceiling set by the state. If a welfare recipient would normally get $300 a month, and pays $150 a month rent, he now gets a check for $450 a month and is supposed to pay the landlord the rent due out of it. If the rent goes up, so will the welfare check. Thus, the welfare tenant really doesn't care how much rent he has to pay, since the city stands ready to increase his check if the rent is raised. But the subject of how much rent is to be charged is left to "negotiation" between the owner of the building and the welfare tenant to whom he is renting. Obviously, this negotiation was a farce, since the tenant would gladly let the owner charge what he wanted so long as the tenant could be confident of full reimbursement through welfare. Only where laws existed controlling rents were landlords stopped from charging what they wished, and even these laws, in New York City, have been substantially weakened in recent years, so as to afford little real constraint on rents in poor areas.[13]

With the Pratt printouts under my arm, I went out to examine the buildings listed to see their condition. The first building I looked at was a seedy rooming house on Empire Boulevard. Its forty apartments were in terrible condition and the hallway reeked of urine. The outside door was broken so I walked right in and began to look around. There were fifteen welfare apartments in the building and twenty-five that were nonwelfare. I scanned the rents paid by each and was astounded. I sat down on the stairwell, disregarded the pungent odors, took out my calculator, and computed the average rents. The welfare families paid rents averaging close to $200 a month per apartment while the nonwelfare families were paying $120 a month for identical apartments. Almost every welfare family was paying more in rent than almost every nonwelfare family in the building.

Obviously, the landlord was charging the welfare

families as much as he possibly could, knowing full well that the city was paying for the apartment while his nonwelfare tenants were bargaining realistically to keep their rents down to levels they could afford. I went to see the landlord and asked him about the rent disparity. "What do you care?" he asked. "They don't pay for it, the city does. Why do you give a damn? It's not their money." The owner was not poor, but he lived off welfare money as surely as did any of his tenants as he overcharges the city for hopelessly inadequate housing. Rental payments to landlords for welfare tenants eat up between a quarter and a third of the money sent each month to welfare recipients. In New York City, for example, about $400 million out of about $1.2 billion sent to welfare recipients goes directly to landlords. Actually, almost one dollar in ten paid landlords for rent in residential New York City apartments comes from welfare monies.[14] The rents welfare tenants pay are astonishingly high. Despite the fact that welfare families are the poorest in New York City and are at the bottom of the socioeconomic ladder, they are still charged rents only 11 percent below the average rent charged a nonwelfare family in New York! Certainly, were full public reimbursement not available for welfare rents, no owner would be able to force such a population as those on welfare to pay so high a rental for dismal living conditions. Indeed, between 1970 and 1973, rents for the welfare population rose 16 percent faster than for the rest of the New York City tenants.[15]

The reason for this rent overcharge lies in the limited number of buildings that will accept welfare tenants. Most landlords resist renting to such families because of their low incomes, large families, and inadequate training or education. They feel that renting to a welfare family is evidence of a building "going downhill," and many see it as a step to take when all hope of maintaining the building over the long term is exhausted and the owner is simply looking for a fast way to maximize his immediate profits on the property. It is hard to find housing for welfare families, and in such a seller's market, landlords are able to charge the city very high rents.

Of course, many of the owners who rent to welfare families are, themselves, politically well connected and may be able to inhibit efforts to contain welfare rents through their political power.

In any event, welfare rents eat up about 35 percent of the welfare grant given the average family (compared to an average rent payment, in New York City, of 25 percent of income).[16] These rents amount to a huge subsidy for the owners of the worst slums in America. The welfare rents are outrageously high, and the living conditions they purchase are unsafe and unhealthy. It would be well if those who spend so much of their time talking about welfare "cheats" spoke instead of the landlords who are daily overcharging the public welfare system. It is their excessive rent charges for terrible housing that represent the most flagrant of the abuses of the welfare system.

SOCIAL SERVICES TO CHILDREN

The Lt. Joseph P. Kennedy, Jr., Home at 1770 Stillwell Avenue in the Bronx in New York City is a foster-care agency, one of the organizations whose budget I studied in my 1977 report for Joint Action for Children. Youngsters who cannot be cared for at home because of the inability of their parents to provide a stable environment are sent to the Kennedy home by the New York City Bureau of Children's Services. It is a private voluntary agency and is reimbursed by the city for the care it provides approximately 300 children.

To care for these 300 children, the Kennedy home employs 267 adults, 7 of whom make more than $20,000 a year. Its staff to "care" for children includes a massive bureaucracy only about half of which works directly with children. One would assume that a virtually one-to-one ratio of staff to children would result in extraordinary care, but foster-care agencies all over New York are constantly criticized for shoddy and inadequate care, amounting to little more than a custodianship rather than part of a program to bring up creative and secure human beings.

The welfare program has come to encompass a vast

secure long-term leases from the city at high rentals, since the health code had so restricted the range of properties that would qualify as potential day-care sites that a scarcity of sites pushed up rents.

Reviewing the impact of staffing and physical facility provisions of the health code concerning day care, McMurray notes, "The result of these twin requirements was to force us to spend huge amounts of money to care for children. Some of the money went to landlords in inflated rents pegged high to meet the costs of conforming to health code restrictions on physical facilities. Some went to meet the salaries commanded by those the health code required us to employ. I am not at all sure that these expenditures had to do with the quality of day care."

The original Johnson administration decision to spend funds on day care and other social services for children has been distorted and perverted to require huge expenditures on overhead, rentals, staff salaries, and bureaucracies. A social service establishment has emerged of landlords, social service agencies, social workers, and welfare administrators committed to high costs and large staffs in all social service areas. Together, they give the impression that funds are spent to provide services to the poor; but really the magnitude of expenditures on social services for children is dictated not by the size of the client population, but by the staffing size, salaries, and rentals built into the system by regulations that work hand in hand with the needs of landlords and social work professionals.

ADMINISTRATIVE COSTS

In the course of my work in 1977 for Joint Action for Children, I examined the impact of the New York City 1977 budget cuts on services to children. Generally, most city services—police, fire, sanitation—had not been cut by very much in the city budget, a reflection of the approaching mayoral election and of increased federal aid under Carter. In all, the 1977-78 budget provided a welcome relief from the days of drastic budget cuts and catastrophic program slashes.

But in children's services the budget cutting continued apace. Expenditures for day care were cut by 10 percent, and funds for foster care were reduced by 3 percent. But when you looked at the rest of the city budget, you found that spending for the *administration* of these services had hardly been cut at all. The Department of Social Services had employed 2,834 people in executive capacities in 1976-77 and was to employ 2,801 in 1977-78. The bureaucracy had taken care of itself while the programs it was to administer had been cut severely.[20]

In all, the city of New York employs 20,223 people to administer its social service programs at a cost of $330 million for salary and fringe benefits. One New York City employee in ten is hired to run the welfare system. Throughout the nation, administrative costs absorb about one third of total cash payments to the poor.

ADMINISTRATIVE COSTS IN WELFARE SERVICES, 1973-74[21]
(in millions)

City	*Cash Payments to Recipients*	*Administrative Costs*	*% Administrative Costs of Cash Payments*
Baltimore	$92	$30	33
Denver	34	11	32
Indianapolis	23	7	30
Norfolk	20	6	30
San Francisco	88	43	49
Washington, D.C.	87	52	60

As pressures have grown to crack down on "welfare cheats" and examine carefully the applications of those seeking new public assistance benefits, bureaucracies have swollen. Such efforts to contain welfare spending often result in little overall drop in expenditures, merely a transfer in the locus of the spending from payments to the poor to payments to bureaucrats. The growth of the welfare bureaucracy is one of the unheralded features of the climb in welfare spending, yet New York City spends as much to run its welfare system as it does to pay benefits of one third of its welfare population, a classic illustration of the bias of the welfare system toward the middle class and against the interests of the poor.

Most people see welfare as a program for the poor. They attribute any increase in the welfare budget to the needs of the poor and blame the liberal social democratic impulse for the cost escalation. In reality, the increase in welfare costs results in no way from increased payments to the poor; these payments have declined, not increased. Rather, it results from the piggybacking onto the basic system of cash payments a network of social and administrative services rendered *by* the middle class *for* the poor. It is the escalation in cost of these services that has caused welfare costs to skyrocket. This growth in spending does not result from any sudden awakening of the social conscience of the northeastern city nor from any sudden surge of demand for service among the poor; it results, rather, from the rapid increase of the charges imposed by the middle class for continuing to render their services to the poor. Some of this increased charge is necessary, but some is profiteering stemming from the shrewd manipulation of the needs of the American city for housing for its poor, services for its children, and integrity in its welfare system. This manipulation is carried on by the real estate interests, the social service agencies, and the welfare system administrators themselves. It is in their ranks that one must search to find the true welfare cheats, not only among the destitute mothers and jobless fathers.

2.

THE MEDICAID MESS

When Joan Slattery walked into the dentist's office with her daughter Mary, the waiting room was packed. Her dentist had recently moved his office to this building and Joan was unaccustomed to seeing so many patients gathered to see him. She approached a stern-looking nurse sitting at a desk squarely in front of the entrance and asked to see the dentist, explaining that she had set an appointment for her daughter. The nurse asked if Joan was eligible for Medicaid (and therefore entitled to free dental care). Joan answered that she was and produced her Medicaid card, which the nurse inspected and asked Joan to have a seat.

Joan soon realized that most of the people in the

waiting room were there to see other doctors having nothing to do with dentistry. Her dentist had joined a group practice, often called a Medicaid mill. After a few minutes, the nurse came over and said, "The podiatrist is on Medicaid too."

Joan wasn't sure the nurse had understood her so she repeated, "No, I wanted to see the dentist."

The nurse grew exasperated: "I know you are here to see the dentist, but it will be a few minutes and I just wanted to tell you that if you want to visit the podiatrist, it is free since he is on Medicaid."

"What would I want with a podiatrist, he's a foot doctor, isn't he?"

"Yes, but he is on Medicaid and I just wanted to tell you that if you wanted to see him, it would not cost you anything and he's available right now."

Joan declined with thanks and then watched the nurse circulate around the waiting room drumming up business for the podiatrist.

Medicaid mills are group practices that cater to patients who are eligible for Medicaid reimbursement for the cost of their care. The Medicaid program, which provides federal and local money for medical treatment of the poor, allows doctors to bill the government for treating Medicaid patients at a flat dollar rate per visit. To maximize the number of visits, and thus the amount of the reimbursement, Medicaid doctors gather together in group practices and refer their patients to one another. This practice, called Ping-Ponging, enables each to claim more patient visits and thus allows them to collect more from Medicaid. A patient may visit the dentist and end up seeing a chiropractor, podiatrist, and allergist, each of whom can then bill the state for a separate patient "visit."

The Medicaid mill is one of the ways in which the medical industry drives up the cost of welfare. Medical care is the leading service provided the poor under the additions to the social welfare program enacted during the Johnson years. It is by far the most expensive of the services provided the poor by the middle class and also the most rapidly growing in cost.

Medical care has traditionally been the last bastion of total private enterprise in America. When President Harry S Truman first proposed a system of national health insurance, the cry of "socialized medicine" rent the air of American politics and has not left it since. During the Kennedy and Johnson administrations, the American Medical Association fought tooth and nail against the Medicaid program of medical assistance to the elderly and the poor. Over their strong-willed and well-financed opposition, the Medicare and Medicaid programs came into being in 1965. Medicare was a fully federally funded program of reimbursement for the treatment of the elderly. Medicaid was designed to provide federal matching grants to states that sought to supplement the Medicare program with their own, more extensive network of aid to the elderly or with a program of assistance to the welfare and working poor. Each state was allowed to file a Medicaid plan with the federal Department of Health, Education, and Welfare incorporating certain eligibility and service standards. States may or may not participate in the Medicaid program—Arizona does not—but if they participate, they must meet stringent federal standards as to the breadth of their plan's coverage and its method of administration to qualify for federal reimbursement.

These federal standards, coupled with lax state administration, have transformed the Medicaid program into a bonanza for the medical profession and a terribly costly program for the northeastern United States. To begin with, federal aid under Medicaid varies depending upon the per capita income of the state. States with a higher per capita income may get only 50% of their costs reimbursed by Washington, whereas states with lower incomes get as much as 80 percent of their costs paid in Washington. The states of the urban Northeast have higher per capita incomes than the rest of the nation and, as a result, get a lesser share of their Medicaid costs reimbursed. Thus, New York, New Jersey, Michigan, Illinois, and Connecticut must be content with only a 50 percent federal reimbursement. In subsequent chapters, we will explore the injustice of using per capita income, unadjusted for regional differences in living costs, as the basis for determining allocations of federal aid. The result of this system is to laden northeastern states with an enormous burden of Medicaid costs, out of all proportion to those in the rest of America. Medicaid costs $180 per capita in New York, $100 in Massachusetts, $80 in Michigan, and $87 in Wisconsin, but in Florida it only costs $24, in North Carolina $37, and in Virginia $41.[1]

Nationally, Medicaid costs more than welfare. In 1975, $12.2 billion was spent by all levels of government to provide medical assistance to the poor, but only $10.8 billion was spent for their welfare benefits.[2] We are thus paying more to keep the poor in medical care than the cost of providing them housing, food, clothing, transportation, and all other living costs combined. In fact, Medicaid costs constitute the fastest growing public budget item in the United States, rising by 48 percent between 1974 and 1977.

Prior to Medicaid, the needs of the poor for medical care went largely unmet, except in rare jurisdictions—New York City among them—where public hospitals provided free care. At first, Medicaid costs swelled as the poor began to go to doctors almost for the first time. Enormous unmet needs were discovered and huge new costs incurred as utilization rose. At the same time, doctors were joining the general mass emigration from the inner city and no longer would set up practices in the ghetto. More and more physicians worked only with hospitals, and it became rare to see a physician in his own office in the core of an American city. Instead, a Medicaid subculture began to emerge as the medical profession tailored its operations and practices to the lucrative reimbursement available under Medicaid. The inner-city private practitioner was replaced by the Medicaid mill offering a group practice to the poor as part of a high-volume trade. Medical schools and hospitals added new equipment and extra beds confident of Medicaid reimbursement for the expenditures. (Today over $5 billion is spent nationally through the two programs for nursing-home care.)[3] A system began to emerge that increased in cost by 20-25 percent each year regardless of any increase in patient demand. In his 1977 State of the State message to the legislature, New York's Governor Hugh L. Carey noted that "Medicaid costs continue to escalate even though the number of beneficiaries is declining and benefit levels have not changed."[4] Even though Medicaid covered the same number of people, and offered the same coverage to each, costs continued to skyrocket.

It is very hard to understand why Medicaid costs keep rising. On the surface, the system seems legitimate enough. Only those eligible for Medicaid can be covered by the program, and the government reimburses health providers for the actual cost of their care. Each hospital, for example, submits to the state government a full accounting of all that it spends for patient care and then the state computes a per diem Medicaid reimbursement rate which it then pays the institution for each day of care of a Medicaid patient. It all seems reasonable and aboveboard. It took me several years to even begin to understand how the overcharges took place.

The turning point for me was a long series of talks with Richard Dresner, now president of the National Center for Telephone Research, a prominent national polling organization, but until 1972, an employee of the federal Social Security Administration, responsible for overseeing the integrity of the Medicare program in New York and New Jersey. "You have to understand that the system is cost-based," he explained. "That means that whatever you pay out in costs, you can get reimbursed by the government. There are few if any real controls over these costs. The state works hard to see to it that the money was actually spent and, in fact, paid out by the health-care provider, but does little to ascertain either that the money should have been spent in the first place or that it was a fair price to pay for the service or product purchased. We would find dozens of nursing homes, for example, in which the owner of the home would bill the state for drugs whose cost was far in excess of the market price and whose need in the particular course of treatment for the patient not at all well established. We would check out the item and would find that the owner had actually bought the drug and had actually paid that inflated price for them. This made him entitled to reimbursement for the drugs. Later, we would find out that the owner of the nursing home had bought real estate somewhere in the West with the owner of the drug company and that the drug company was funneling back a portion of the excess sales price of the drugs to the nursing-home operator through the real estate venture."[5]

Some of this excessive billing is criminal, and there have been dozens of incidents and convictions of nursing-home operators in New York, Rhode Island, Massachusetts, and other states. But even legitimate providers of medical care get caught up in the system. As Dresner explained, "If you run a hospital and you want to build a new wing, or get some fancy new equipment, or hire more nurses, you can go right ahead since you know that these costs will all become part of your submission to Medicaid. You will get your money back from Medicaid even if all else fails. It is an incentive to dramatic and rapid expansion of the medical industry."

The key is to understand the notion of "fixed costs." Some medical care costs rise and fall as more or fewer patients are admitted, whereas others—such as those for administration, overhead, construction, equipment acquisition, and the like—remain constant regardless of how many patients are treated. A recent study in Ohio indicated that these "fixed costs" constitute about 70 percent of the total hospital bill.[6] When Medicaid reimburses a hospital for its "costs," it must pay for these fixed charges as well as the direct costs of treating a particular patient. But the state has little control over what these fixed costs are. Hospitals must obtain a certificate of need for planned expansion from state health departments and, in different states, need state approval for acquisition of new equipment. But state health agencies are usually loath to deny this permission, and often the requirement of public approval is more pro forma than real.

Says James Posner, former deputy director of Medicaid in New York City, "Even with certificate of need approval, Health Services Administration approval, and Article 20 review, it is still exceedingly easy for health providers to add to their fixed costs. It is quite difficult for a public body to assess how badly needed a certain piece of equipment really is."[7] Hospitals that should remain community hospitals become medical centers. Heart-lung machines that are not needed are acquired; empires are built, reputations advanced, and careers made. Medicaid pays for a lot of legitimate care, but it also pays for much ego building and medical status symbols.

The irony and anomaly of the fixed-cost system of Medicaid billing is that it doesn't make a great deal of difference how many people receive medical care. Dresner once explained to me, "Most public agencies look in the wrong direction when they try to regulate Medicaid. They look at how to control patient utilization or Medicaid eligibility. They try to keep poor people from using medical facilities quite as much or to restrict the definition of who is poor enough to qualify for Medicaid. All this means is that the rate per patient actually treated by a hospital goes up. The fixed costs don't decline just because fewer patients use the facilities. They are just spread over fewer patients so that the state ends up paying that much more for each one."

State governments are understandably concerned about the rapid increases in Medicaid costs. Through my work as a consultant to the speaker of the New York State Assembly, Stanley Steingut, I have spent hundreds of hours trying to explain the relevance of fixed costs to Medicaid charges. Unfortunately, too much emphasis is placed by states on controlling the utilization of Medicaid facilities by the poor. Even as legislators ponder new ways to assure that only those who need medical care receive it, hospitals can continue to acquire new equipment, add new facilities, and build in new costs of care. We deal with a hybrid system, part public, part private. The public sector must stand ready to reimburse all the costs of care rendered by the private sector, but has little real control over the decisions made by the private sector that determine how much that care is to cost.

In a very real sense, the Medicaid budget is nominally in the control of state and local governments, but is actually more of a blank check for the providers of health-care services. Unfortunately, the poor are blamed for these costs. We don't call Medicaid a "subsidy to a hospital"; rather we call it a "subsidy to the poor." We blame the liberal social impulse that created Medicaid for its rapid cost excalation rather than the exploitation of the program by the medical industry. We assume that Medicaid cost increases reflect increased "give-aways" to the poor, when all they reflect is increased subsidy to those who make their living providing medical care to the poor.

MEDICAL SCHOOLS AND MEDICAID

New York University School of Medicine stands aloof and austere on Thirty-second Street and First Avenue in Manhattan. Close to the apex of the medical establishment, its corridors are quiet, dignified, and serious. Each year, the school sends forth 185 graduates who are among the cream of the nation's medical profession. Nearby on Twenty-seventh Street and First Avenue stands Bellevue Hospital. Its corridors are noisy, its tone urgent, and its understaffing evident. New York City Comptroller Harrison J. Goldin once told me that "if I were ill in the back of an ambulance, and they were taking me to Bellevue, I would lean forward, rap on the window of the ambulance cab, and plead, 'Drive a little longer, take me to Mount Sinai or Beth Israel, don't take me to Bellevue.' "

The bulk of Bellevue's budget comes from Medicaid. It is a hospital for the poor. New York University School of Medicine is a school for the nation's elite. But Bellevue subsidizes the New York University School of Medicine through its Medicaid program. This floundering medical institution—Bellevue Hospital—is a key prop in the financial structure that holds up New York University School of Medicine as one of the nation's finest. This subsidy comes through the "affiliation" of Bellevue with NYU Medical School. NYU provides much of the staff for Bellevue and uses the hospital to educate its students. Bellevue reimburses NYU for this staff time with funds it gets from the Medicaid program. This affiliation provides Bellevue with a staff much more qualified than it would be able to attract on its own, but results in costs of treatment and care that are much higher than would be the case were Bellevue not used as an educational facility. Typically, medical students follow the faculty on their patient rounds, asking questions and learning, from a practical viewpoint, about the medical theory they are taught in the classroom. But this teaching is expensive. The average cost per day of patient care in a hospital affiliated with a medical school is $161.88, whereas the average cost of the nonaffiliated hospital is only $109.33.[8] Much of this increased cost is due to the extra costs of teaching while medical care is provided. It is impossible to pinpoint how much of the greater cost in teaching hospitals is due to teaching and how much to the fact that teaching hospitals often tend to be better or at least better-equipped hospitals. Nevertheless, when the patient treated by a teaching hospital is a Medicaid patient, Medicaid must pay this extra cost of teaching.

In this way, state and local taxpayers must bear a share of medical education costs having little or nothing to do with actual service to the poor. They have no choice in the matter. As local government participates in the Medicaid program, it is obliged to pay for all reasonable costs incurred in treating those who are eligible for Medicaid, and no distinction is effectively made between money spent for teaching and money spent for medical care. Medicaid must subsidize medical education. As a result, huge portions of the Medicaid expenditures of state and local governments—and the resulting taxes on their citizens—have to do with subsidies to medical schools, not with subsidies to the poor. There is, of course, nothing wrong with subsidizing medical education, but let's call it a subsidy to medical education and debate whether the subsidy is an appropriate task of local government or a truly federal obligation. Let's not call it Medicaid and lump it under the welfare budget. It is not the poor who are benefiting from the subsidy; it is the medical student. It is not the New Deal, liberal impulse that is impelling the payment; it is society's desire to augment the ranks of doctors available to us all. But through the concealment of medical education subsidies in the Medicaid budget, we mistakenly take the costs of providing medical care to the poor as higher than they actually are or need be.

The taxpayers of the Northeast pay a disproportionate share of this Medicaid subsidy for medical education. In the first place, the northeastern cities have the largest number of teaching hospital beds in the nation. New York, Pennsylvania, and New Jersey, for example, have almost 50 percent more teaching hospital beds per capita of population than the rest of the country.[9] Thus, the concentration of medical schools, especially high-quality schools, in the northeastern city is reflected in a concentration of teaching hospital beds. It is this disproportionately high ratio of teaching beds that is a key part of the reason for the higher Medicaid costs borne by the northeastern city and the northeastern urban taxpayer.

The graduates of NYU Medical School and all the quality northeastern urban medical schools work all over America. As the nation's hub of medical education, the northeastern city trains the nation's doctors. Not only must the Northeast pay for more medical education than must the rest of America, but it gets less federal reimbursement. As noted earlier, the northeastern states generally get only 50 percent federal reimbursement under Medicaid, whereas some southern states get as much as 80 percent. To force Medicaid to pay for much of this schooling and then to reimburse this Medicaid expenditure to a lesser extent than is afforded in the rest of the nation is a particularly unusual injustice. The net effect of the increased costs of medical education and the inflationary impact on Medicaid of hospital equipment acquisition has been to drive up the hospital costs of the urban Northeast beyond all proportion to the rest of America. The cost of medical education is centered primarily in the northeastern city because it is in these cities that the nation's top medical schools are located. The hospitals with which they affiliate add the costs of education and the costs of the equipment and machinery they must purchase to gratify the needs of education to their fixed-cost base for Medicaid reimbursement. As a result, the cost of a day of hospital care in an American city is $123.61, whereas in rural communities it is just $81.85. As the following table indicates, these higher costs are almost exclusively concentrated in the northeastern states and cities as opposed to their Sun Belt or southern counterparts:

HOSPITAL COSTS PER PATIENT-DAY[10]

Northeast		Sun Belt	
City	*Costs per Patient-Day*	*City*	*Costs per Patient-Day*
Boston	$233.64	Atlanta	$136.18
Chicago	153.03	Dallas	108.96
Cleveland	136.21	Houston	117.48
Detroit	166.01	Jacksonville	123.83
Indianapolis	126.70	Nashville	108.55
Milwaukee	140.20	New Orleans	113.52
New York	168.25	Phoenix	138.52
Philadelphia	136.88	San Antonio	111.40
AVERAGE	$157.63	AVERAGE	$119.81

Urban United States: $123.61
Rural United States: $81.85

Hospital costs are about one-third higher in the largest northern cities than in the largest Sun Belt cities and about 50 percent higher in metropolitan than in nonmetropolitan areas. These cost differences are substantial and have an important impact on Medicaid rates.

NURSING HOMES: A STUDY IN PROFITING FROM NEGLECT

Carol Rattner is a nurse at Brooklyn Jewish Hospital, the facility to which patients were transferred from the Willoughby Nursing Home when they developed a need for intensive medical care. The Willoughby Home at 949 Willoughby Avenue in Brooklyn is owned by Bernard Bergman, reportedly the owner of scores of nursing homes, recently convicted of conspiracy, tax fraud, and bribery in connection with his nursing home empire.

Rattner describes the condition of patients from the Willoughby Home: "... they were almost always severely dehydrated, malnourished, semi-comatose, lethargic, confused, and disoriented and had elevated temperatures and large decubiti [bedsores] with pus-like draining.

"In one instance a female patient, I recall, came in from Willoughby with an apparent respiratory infection. This was treated, successfully, at this hospital, and she returned to Willoughby. She was soon returned to this hospital with the same apparent symptoms, i.e., dehydration, malnutrition, and infection."[11]

In 1974 and 1975, inspired by the crusading reporting of Jack Newfield, stories like this one appeared in the pages of *The Village Voice* and, through the efforts largely of John Hess, in *The New York Times*. They were typical of the gross neglect and outrageous indifference to human life that characterize the operation of nursing homes throughout the United States. The outcry that flowed from these exposés was so intense that a special prosecutor was created in New York State to bring indictments against key figures in the nursing home scandal.

Amid the furor about illegal and unethical practice in these long-term care facilities, we miss one basic point: The illegalities are scarcely necessary to make money. The very system of nursing homes itself allows for reaping unconscionable profits without the violation of any statute, regulation, or administrative order. The months since the uncovering of massive patient abuse in nursing home operation have been filled with investigations, recriminations, and indictments. But little has been done to alter the basic system itself which permits vast profits, exorbitant costs, and inadequate care without any illegality.

To begin with, most of the patients in nursing homes don't need to be there in the first place. A 1973 study by the New York City Health Services Administration estimated that one third of the patients in long-term nursing beds did not need such care and would be better off in their own homes.[12] Congressman Edward I. Koch of New York has proposed legislation extending the program of home care and keeping patients who do not need such care out of nursing homes. Nevertheless, the system is so structured that patients who have no need of nursing home care end up there anyway. The law often gives them no choice.

When an elderly person finds that she cannot manage the shopping and housekeeping by herself, she often looks to hire a homemaker or other aide to assist her. Since she normally cannot afford such assistance on her own, she usually comes to Medicaid to ask for help. There she runs into a nightmare. The Medicaid people look at her income and assets and tell her that she cannot qualify for Medicaid. "But," she says, "if I strip myself of these assets and lower my income, I cannot afford to live on my own, and if I don't do so, I can't get Medicaid and then I can't afford to hire the homemaker I need to be able to live alone." It's a Catch-22. Damned if you do, damned if you don't. She often has no choice but to enter a nursing home even though all she needs is a person a few hours a day to clean up or cook or shop. The city ends up paying fifty or sixty dollars a day to pay for her nursing home while all she needs is ten dollars worth of home care.[13]

How can she finance the nursing home? Through "spending down." The nursing home takes the elderly person's assets and sells them to pay for the nursing home care. When she is destitute, the home just applies for Medicaid for her and collects the rest of the bill from Medicaid. Of course, this leaves the senior citizen impoverished and devoid of any assets with which to live alone. All she may once have needed was a homemaker, but now she is getting sixty dollars a day of care that she doesn't need and has been stripped of assets that would allow her to be independent.

The very basis of the nursing home system is that private, profit-making practitioners perform services and receive for them full reimbursement. But the system has no accurate way of checking:

- whether the patients need the care they are to receive;
- whether the care given was adequate;
- whether the costs incurred in rendering the care were reasonable.

Current practice entails the periodic audit of a nursing home to determine if treatment was excessive and costs reasonable. But these audits are limited because of the severe constraints on the capacity of state health agencies to hire inspectors. More to the point, when an audit reveals a malpractice, the state can only recover the actual cost of the overcharge or bad treatment discovered. It cannot proceed to collect a larger amount of money based on other likely instances of the same bad practice, since it does not have concrete evidence of the abuse. The nursing home operator is paid on presentation of his bills. It is only months or years later that a small portion of these billings are evaluated. Even if all are found to be faulty, state health departments lack the manpower or the time to review the other billings to determine their authenticity.

Often, even when the state develops enough data to close down a nursing home, it has no way to collect its money back. Excessive billings may be clear, but when the money has already been spent and paid to vendors, there is little real prospect of recovery for the state. Sometimes the nursing home owner is really just a dummy corporation—an instrument of the real owner but not the owner himself. In some such instances, the actual "owner" is really a consortium of suppliers who sell drugs, food, clothing, linen, and other products and services to the nursing home at inflated prices. To proceed against the nominal owner of such a nursing home is to miss the point and let the real culprits go free.

The state of the art of nursing home regulation lags far behind the state of the art of nursing home chicanery. Yet nursing home care currently consumes one Medicaid dollar in three. Nationally, $5.2 billion is spent on nursing homes, over $500 million of it in New York City itself. Almost every impartial investigation of the nursing home industry has found it to be laden with corruption, poor treatment, and overcharge. The magnitude of these larcenies is enormous and has a decidedly inflationary impact on state and local budgets, particularly in the Northeast where the bulk of these nursing homes are concentrated.

In New York City nursing care reimbursement rates run up to one hundred dollars a day for each patient, a cost that exceeds even that of acute, intensive care in most rural hospitals. Clearly, Medicaid costs have gotten out of hand. We have recognized clearly in recent years the extent of criminality in the nursing home industry and, through New York's appointment of a special prosecutor, have hopes of dealing with the problem at least in New York State. But the basic *noncriminal* abuses of the system—unnecessary care, inadequate treatment, inflated costs, and sweetheart relationships between purchasers and sellers of goods and services—all remain uncorrected. Together, they constitute a constant and substantial drain on public revenues. Money paid for nursing homes appears to be flowing to meet the medical needs of the elderly poor. It is traditionally included in what the public has come to regard as social welfare spending. But, as before, these costs are attributable neither to the real needs of the poor nor to the desires of liberals that these needs be met. They are due, instead, to the exploitation of the needs of the poor by profit-hungry nursing home operators, an exploitation that continues unabated to this day.

MEDICAID MILL

Another species of medical practice, the Medicaid mill, is a source of major abuse and overcharging. The most thorough investigation of Medicaid mills was undertaken in 1976 by the Subcommittee on Longer Term Care of the United States Senate Committee on Aging, chaired by the former senator from Utah, Frank Moss. In an inquiry that featured Moss dressed up as a welfare client entering Medicaid mills in New York City, the subcommittee uncovered devastating evidence of fraud and exploitation of the Medicaid program by doctors.[14]

The Senate report defined a Medicaid mill as "a hole in the wall located in a dilapidated part of town. A few have large plate windows, but most are solid brick without windows or with windows boarded.... Most mills are single story facilities not infrequently the ground floor of former residential buildings.... It appears that these facilities would not survive without Medicaid. Repeatedly, in our investigation, the staff learned of now-prosperous participants in the Medicaid program who could never find a practice before the proliferation of Medicaid mills. For example, three New York chiropractors who ultimately formed a partnership which gave them ownership of a half dozen facilities and an income of $500,000 a year each had been unable to find work in their profession until the enactment of Medicaid."

The outpatient practice of Medicaid is cornered by a few doctors whose practices cater to Medicaid reimbursement. In New York, 7 percent of the physicians earned 50 percent of the Medicaid fees paid to doctors. In Michigan 3 percent earned 25 percent of the Medicaid fees.[15]

Senator Moss, on the morning of June 7, 1976, entered a Medicaid mill at 145 East 116th Street dressed in "the worst looking clothes I could find." The senator complained of a cold and posed as a patient. After a brief examination by a participating doctor, Moss was asked if he had a fever and replied that he did not. The senator was asked if he had an arthritic condition. Although he replied that he had not, the doctor referred him to a chiropractor on the grounds that he might have a muscle spasm. Before the beknighted senator had left the clinic, he had received a urine test, a blood test, a chest Xray, had his neck twisted, was given a variety of drug prescriptions, and had a picture taken of his cervical spine.

The purpose of this runaround is clear: For each visit with a patient and each test or Xray, the Medicaid doctor receives separate reimbursement. By passing patients from doctor to doctor, the reimbursements mount and each doctor can bill separately. Since doctors practice individually under the Medicaid law and group practices are not recognized as such in most states, the Medicaid program regulators have no idea that the patient is being referred to the various stops in the mill.

Cities with Medicaid mills spend millions of dollars on this totally inadequate care. About a quarter of the total Medicaid budget in New York City—over $400 million—is spent on outpatient medical care, much of it flowing to Medicaid mills of the sort investigated by Senator Moss.

The Medicaid mill is the successor to the ghetto doctor. In years past, private practitioners located in individual offices in the inner city tended to their patients as best they could. A combination of crime, deteriorating social conditions, and growing poverty made the private, individual practice of medicine in the inner city an impossibility. Doctors fled to the suburbs or to the hospital-based setting. As a result, the demand for treatment in outpatient clinics of urban hospitals mushroomed, growing from 1.4 million visits per year in 1974 to 1.7 million visits per year in 1975 in New York's municipal hospitals. Unfortunately, hospital outpatient visits came to be very expensive, each visit costing not only the actual costs of treatment but also the allocated part of that hospital's "fixed costs." To develop an alternative to outpatient hospital visits, group practices of private doctors, unaffiliated with any hospital, sprang up throughout the inner city. State health departments generally set a fixed rate—seven dollars or five dollars—for each visit to these private doctors. In doing so, the state avoided the necessity of fixing any cost-based rate of payment, which would have required a separate audit of each doctor's books. Regrettably, in doing so, the state placed a premium on a volume practice and high patient turnover. The more patients a doctor saw, regardless of the quality of care, the more wealthy he became. Rather than minimize patient visits, as most health providers seek to do, Medicaid mill doctors sought to maximize them and, through their group practice, to "Ping-Pong" them from one doctor to the other. Medicaid mills are virtually unregulated. Until recently, few state health departments even knew how many Medicaid mills existed in their own states or how they operated. But even today, little is being done to crack down on these mills, and the situation, in New York for example, is as bad as it was when Senator Moss initiated his inquiry in 1976.

It is these leeches on the Medicaid budget—Medicaid mills, nursing homes, medical education, and excessive acquisition of beds and equipment by hospitals—that suck away funds intended for the genuine medical needs of the poor. Like one giant gravy bowl, the Medicaid program meets the financial needs of a host of service providers quite irrespective of how well these services meet the medical needs of the poor. The resulting rapid increase in Medicaid costs is a key element in the increasing strain to which northeastern urban state and local budgets are being subjected. Even so conservative a spokesman as former Treasury Secretary William Simon called Medicaid "the root of the New York City fiscal crisis."[16]

It is indeed at the root of the problem. As long as Medicaid remains an essentially unpoliced public repayment of privately incurred expenses without subjecting these private expenditures to adequate controls and prior approvals, Medicaid will drain funds from urban budgets at an alarming pace. For our purposes, however, it is important to note that through Medicaid and through the purchase-of-services elements of the welfare program, our cities are losing the funds originally allocated to aid the poor. But it is not the poor nor even the politically progressive forces that would aid those who are causing this drain of urban dollars. It is neither the needs of the former nor the ideology of the latter that is escalating welfare and Medicaid expenditures to the point where they break the back of the urban budget. It is the exploitation of the welfare and Medicaid program by service providers that forces up its cost. If we are to contain the costs of welfare and Medicaid and bring them to a level that is fiscally acceptable, we must isolate the welfare cheats and purge them from the rolls. But it is primarily among the ranks of the middle-class service providers in which we must look for them, not among the poor.

3.

THE BANK STRIKE

The gross national product of Belgium is $39 billion, that of Greece is $13 billion, Norway's is $16 billion, and Mexico's $40 billion. The total assets of the First National City Bank of New York—Citibank—are $61 billion, larger than that of any of these nations. Citibank might as well be a separate country. Its capitol is located at Fifty-third Street and Lexington Avenue. It employs 47,000 people in five hundred branches throughout the world. It is only one of the major New York banks (together the New York City commercial banks have combined assets approaching $200 billion, more than the gross national product of all but a handful of countries).

America's cities depend on banks for their survival. It

is one of the less publicized but more elemental facts of urban finance that cities survive financially only as banks permit. Neither the state nor the federal government is nearly as important to the city as are the banks. Ultimately, whether a city administration succeeds or fails relates a lot more to how well a mayor can get along with the banks than how well he can relate to unions, political leaders, or even the electorate.

Cities depend on banks in two different ways:

- When cities wish to build schools, housing, libraries, parks, sewers, or make other capital improvements, the cost of the construction is usually too great to permit them to absorb the full amount in any single year's budget. Cities can only undertake such construction if they are able to spread the cost of the construction over the life of the improvement. A new school might be used for thirty or forty years. Cities finance the construction of the school by borrowing to pay for it and then repaying the loan over the life of the school—one-thirtieth or one-fortieth each year. Unless cities can borrow the money for construction initially, they cannot hope to keep pace with their need for new capital facilities that their citizens require.
- Cities get their revenue from two major sources: locally imposed taxes and aid from state, county, or federal governments and agencies. Neither of these forms of revenue flows to cities in fifty-two equal installments, one each week. Some taxes are collected quarterly, others annually. Some federal or state aid programs only give cities the money at the end of the year. Yet cities must meet their expenses constantly. Personnel, the largest city expense item, must be paid weekly or biweekly, as must welfare recipients and others. Contractors who work for a city must also be paid regularly, as must other claimants on the city treasury. To reconcile the irregular flow of cash into the city treasury with the regular flow of cash out of it, all cities must borrow throughout the year, repaying these loans with cash they get in taxes or in aid

> later in the year. Such loans are called "short term"; the capital loans discussed earlier are called "long term."

Banks are the key to municipal borrowing. They can lend cities the money they require directly and receive bonds or notes (bonds for long term and notes for short term) in exchange for the loans. Banks can also "underwrite" the city's loans by buying the bonds and then reselling them to individual or other institutional lenders who buy bonds for their own use. It is not feasible for the city to borrow directly from hundreds and thousands of individuals or businesses. They are too numerous and a city's access to the financial community too limited. It is with and through banks that the bulk of bonds are sold, with the bank acting as either the direct lender or the underwriter.

Banks find their transactions with cities immensely profitable. City bonds are generally backed by a constitutional requirement that the promise of repayment they contain be met. In most cases, the holder of a city bond has the right to go to court and force a city to honor its repayment commitment even before any other city expense—including police and fire salaries—is met. During the recent fiscal crisis in New York City, this legal commitment was tested several times in the courts and each time bills passed by the New York State Legislature delaying repayment were ruled unconstitutional by the courts and prompt payment ordered to note and bond holders.

City bonds have the additional advantage of being tax exempt; that is, the interest earned on them may not be subjected to federal income taxation. For a wealthy investor, this substantially augments the value of the bond, since he can avoid paying taxes on the interest, no matter how high his tax bracket. If he is in a 50 percent tax bracket, for example, and buys an 8 percent city bond, his real yield is 12 percent, since he need not pay taxes on his interest.

Banks have traditionally found, through the purchase of tax-exempt bonds, that they can lower substantially the tax they must pay as corporations. When this tax-exempt feature of city bonds (and state or county bonds as well) is combined with the security afforded by their constitutional guarantee of repayment, such lending has always been highly profitable to banks. When banks choose to underwrite a bond issue (that is, resell it to investors) rather than buy the bonds and add them to the banks' own portfolio of investments, the bank is really acting as a broker, buying and reselling the bonds for a commission of one quarter or one half of 1 percent. Since each year about $17 billion of state, county, and local bonds are sold, a commission of one quarter to one half of 1 percent would yield a lucrative income of over $40 million a year for the underwriter, a profit that is earned by little work and even less risk (if worse comes to worse, the bank just adds the bond to its own portfolio).[1]

Historically, the profitability of local bonds led to a cozy relationship between banks and cities. Banks could not get enough city bonds and notes, and rarely did a bond or note issue remain on the market for more than a few hours. In 1971, for example, 59 percent of all state and local bonds issues were bought by commercial banks, eager for the tax exemption and the security of the issues.

But by 1973 this close relationship began to sour in the eyes of the banking community. For a variety of reasons, banks cut back sharply their purchases of local bonds. Whereas in 1971 they had purchased $12.8 billion in local bonds, they bought only $7.1 billion in 1972 and a mere $3.9 billion in 1973.[2] The reasons for this precipitous falloff in the traditionally large state and local bond purchases of the commercial banks will never fully be known, as it is buried away in the secret meetings of top-level bank decision makers. But several factors appear to have contributed to their decision to stop lending to American cities:

- Borrowing by the business community, the favorite clients of the banks, rose sharply. American commercial banks lent corporations only $3.8 billion in 1971, but lent $19.2 billion in 1972 and $29.7 billion in 1973.[3] This growth in business borrowing came largely at the expense of states and localities, formerly the largest bank customers.

- Increasingly, commercial banks found other ways to shield their assets from federal taxation. Through the location of branches abroad, they were able to shelter their profits and cut their federal tax liability without buying state and local bonds. As commercial banks catered to the needs of the huge multinational corporations, it became possible to accept deposits outside the United States and never run afoul of federal tax regulations. In a sense, multinational corporations gave what cities and states used to possess exclusively, the right to shelter capital from federal taxation.
- Concern about the social erosion of cities and their increasing malaise led commercial banks to hedge their bets and decrease sharply their inventories of state and local bonds, not just in the urban Northeast, but throughout the country.

The result of the commercial banks' refusal to buy bonds starting in 1973 was to switch the nature of the market upon which cities were forced to rely. No longer could huge blocks of city bonds and notes be bought by a few banks for their own portfolio, but, instead, large sales had to be held aiming at the far more volatile and less controllable market of individual investors. Banks still accepted bonds and notes, not for their own portfolio, but for resale to other investors, notably to individuals. In 1972 individual holders of state and city bonds and notes throughout the nation actually *sold* \$1.6 billion more of these bonds and notes than they bought. But in 1973, under prodding from banks and aggressive marketing, they bought \$5.5 billion more than they sold. The banks withdrew from the market for state and local bonds and let the individual investor take up the slack.[4]

The withdrawal was a silent one. No press releases were issued, no newspaper columns written. Nobody wanted to rock the boat and say anything that might scare away the individual investor and shake his faith in the security of state and local bonds by scare stories to the effect that banks were now eschewing these bonds. Banks wanted the individual investor to buy as much as possible so that they could reap the one quarter to one half of 1 percent underwriting fee from the sale of these notes and bonds and so that they could sell bonds and notes they had bought in years past at a profit.

But as the nature of the bond-buying market changed from institutional to individual, so did the fiscal basis of the American city. No longer were cities able to borrow directly from local banks; banks were no longer buying city notes and bonds as part of their commitment to their home city. Rather, banks had abandoned the city. They became headquarters-less, international institutions without roots and without loyalty. The banks who had been sustained by the deposits of residents of these cities and states absolved themselves of any loyalty and ceased to be involved in the fiscal affairs of their native cities except as underwriters. Their place was taken by individual investors who didn't feel any loyalty to the particular city or state whose bonds they bought (many bought bonds of cities and states in which they did not live and to which they owed no allegiance at all). Rather, these new investors were attracted by the lure of high interest rates exempt from federal taxation. These investors had no roots in the city or state in which they invested and felt under no obligation to sustain them.

The swing in bank investment from cities to businesses that took place during the prosperous times of 1973 was not necessarily permanent. Many times before, as the economy perked up, corporate and business loan demand had increased, attracting bank funds away from city and state bond issues. There was nothing necessarily new in this trend. Usually, during these prosperous times, state and city borrowing needs are easily met by the many new, high-tax-bracket investors eager for state and local tax-exempt bonds. Prosperity may deny cities the funds of the banks, now attracted to corporate borrowers, but it replaces them with high-bracket investors eager to shelter their newly increased incomes from taxation with state and local tax-exempt notes and bonds.

But in 1975 the national economy began to slide again into recession and depression. Business loan demand fell off and no longer were corporations clamoring for capital from commercial banks. In 1974 corporations borrowed from commercial banks $31 billion more than they repaid, but in 1975 they repaid $12.4 billion more than they borrowed. With business in the throes of an economic slump, banks were faced with the choice: buy more state and local bonds or find new loan customers.[5]

The federal government came to the rescue. Between 1972 and 1974, federal borrowings had been relatively constant, ranging between $20 and $23 billion a year. In 1975, under the impact of the largest peacetime deficit in American history, federal borrowing soared to $83 billion. Banks could now continue to turn their backs on the cities in which they were located and lend their money instead to the federal government. Indeed, federal borrowing from commercial banks skyrocketed from –$3.8 billion in 1974 to +$29.6 billion in 1975. Whereas banks have historically absorbed 23 percent of federal borrowing, in 1975 they absorbed 36 percent of federal borrowing, a record amount.[6]

Thus, even with the falloff in business borrowing, banks continued their headlong rush away from the state and local bond market, cutting their purchases of local bonds from $5.7 billion in 1974 to a mere $2.4 billion in 1975. Banks that had accounted for 59 percent of all municipal bond sales in 1971 accounted for only 15 percent in 1975.[7]

Banks had given up on the American city. In good times, they would rather lend to business and in bad times they would rather lend to the federal government. The one sine qua non was: Never lend to cities.

Finally, the bank boycott of the cities could not be kept secret. As the bottom fell out of the economy in 1975, individual investors were no longer eager to snap up any municipal bonds or notes that came onto the market. Recession and depression had dried up their reserves of capital in need of the tax shelter afforded by state and local bonds and notes; cities found it more and more difficult to find borrowers. Those cities most in need of capital and in the shakiest financial condition succumbed first. But all cities found that they had to scrounge for capital as they had never been forced to do before.

New York City was uniquely vulnerable. Its budget had been stretched to the breaking point by years of deficit spending, and its capital needs were immense. Indeed, New York's sheer volume of financial need sent tremors through the financial community. By mid-1975, it became evident that New York City was finding it difficult, if not impossible, to find lenders at almost any interest rate. A panic developed which led to a total closure of the credit market to New York City bonds and notes. Soon all cities in New York State, including the state government itself, were in jeopardy of losing access to the capital market.

Cut off from credit, the New York City default crisis began to attract national attention. From then on the flow of events is amply and publicly recorded: New York State intervened and set up the Municipal Assistance Corporation to sell bonds on behalf of New York City and guarantee those bonds through interception of sales and stock transfer tax revenues. When investors grew wary of even the Municipal Assistance Corporation, the Emergency Financial Control Board was established by the New York State Legislature to monitor and control the activities of New York City to assure their fiscal prudence. When even this failed to stem the panic concerning New York City's ability to repay its debt, the federal government, after much urging and over Gerald Ford's initial refusal, undertook to lend New York the money it required for a three-year period in return for a commitment by the city, reinforced by the Emergency Financial Control Board, to balance the city budget over three years.

When the fiscal crisis first hit and default threatened, the banks pointed their finger at the New York City administration. They contended that years of liberal mismanagement had so snarled city finances that no lender in his or her right mind would extend credit to the city. They charged that welfare spending and fiscal manipulations coupled with giveaways to city unions had fouled the city's fiscal nest almost beyond repair and intoned piously that they could not, in good conscience, commit more of their depositors' money to such a fiscal nightmare. By and large, the bank line was accepted. It did more than anything else to foster the sentiment that it was liberalism and misguided social conscience that had caused the fiscal crisis. Businessmen joined the chorus for a return to conservative fiscal verities of a balanced budget and reduced spending.

But, as George Bernard Shaw once said, "History will tell lies as usual." The fact is that the banks stopped lending the cities of America money long before the fiscal crisis in New York had set in. Their refusal to lend cities money dates from 1973, not from 1975 when the fiscal crisis surfaced. The bank refusal to lend money extended well beyond the borders of New York City or Yonkers or Newark but ran to almost every American state or city of any size. What had happened was not an attack of fiscal conservatism that caused banks to stop extending credit to cities, but rather a desire to shunt their capital first to business and then to the federal government which caused, in turn, the fiscal crisis. *Cities* did not cause the fiscal crisis that New York suffered in 1975; *banks* did. Obviously, without the basic fiscal irresponsibility of many cities, including New York, the fiscal crisis need not have been as severe as it actually was, but the trigger to the default crisis was the bank boycott, not the innate irresponsibility itself.

The balance of this book will examine why city finances became so ensnarled. As it will show, their instability is due more to federal than to local policies, more to national than to urban trends. But the question remains, Why did banks withdraw from cities? Why did they choose federal and business loans over state and local investment?

Undoubtedly, part of the answer lies in their decreased need for the tax exemption afforded by state and local bonds given the availability to the banks of foreign capital generated by multinational corporate depositors beyond the reach of the United States tax law. But many have speculated that a more sinister motive lay behind the bank decision in 1973 to boycott state and local bond issues. Banks may well have decided that the earnings they could achieve through underwriting state and local bond issues, as opposed to absorbing them in their own portfolios, would be substantial yet would still permit banks to invest their own capital in the more profitable corporate bonds to which they switched in 1973. Implicit in the bank move away from state and local bonds and notes was a decision to set in motion a scarcity in the bond market that would drive up the interest rate of bonds and notes. When the commercial banks, who had bought 59 percent of all state and local bonds and notes in 1971 and 55 percent in 1972, bought only 28 percent in 1973, they must have realized that the resulting scarcity of lenders would force cities to offer bonds and notes at higher interest rates. Banks may well have decided that they could increase their earnings on the state and local bonds they eventually did buy while decreasing the amount of their capital tied up in such investment, all the time reaping the underwriting profit that would accrue from their role as seller of state and local bonds to the balance of the market. By their decision to use their influence over the bond market to create a scarcity of bond purchasers, the banks, in effect, created a higher interest rate which assured them a larger profit on the smaller volume of state and local bonds they would buy while releasing their funds for investment in corporate and later federal paper.

The end result of this process of fiscal manipulation is that New York City today staggers under a debt service burden that is larger than any other item in the city budget. Indeed, the interest on the debt that city taxpayers must pay is larger than the total of all public assistance payments to the poor (excluding that for rent) in any year.[8] Interest rates for all American cities have jumped as a result of the bank boycott of the American city. Philadelphia, for example, had to pay a 9 percent interest rate at the height of the New York crisis, and other cities find their interest costs dramatically higher than in the early part of this decade.

Into the vacuum created by the bank boycott of city notes and bonds stepped a number of new purchasers for city and state paper. Some merely sought higher interest rates for their capital. These included individual investors (9 percent of the market), municipal bond funds—aggregates of individual and institutional investors (22 percent of the market)—and personal and common bank trust funds (8 percent of the market).[9] These investors sought high yields and tax shelters, and their needs could be gratified at great cost to city and federal taxpayers.

But other purchasers stepped into the market whose motives for the purchase of state and local bonds and notes were more suspect: casualty insurance companies, savings banks, and municipal union pension funds. All three have one thing in common: They are closely regulated by state or local government. Their sudden interest in making loans to state and local governments raises the serious question of whether they were investing money or tendering a bribe to the governments that regulated them. The rapidity of the increase in purchase of state and local notes and bonds by pension funds, insurance companies, and savings banks is suspect indeed. In 1971 these three sources accounted for 17 percent of the state and local bonds sold in America; in 1977 they will account for 43 percent—more than twice as much. The increase is a dramatic one:

STATE AND LOCAL SECURITIES PURCHASED BY PENSION FUNDS, INSURANCE COMPANIES, AND SAVINGS BANKS[10]

Investing Institutions	% of All Securities Sold	
	1971	*1977*
Municipal union pension funds	0*	8
Casualty insurance companies	16	24
Savings banks and savings and loan associations	1	11
TOTAL	17	43

**In 1971 municipal union pension funds sold off more bonds than they bought.*

The increase in the purchase of state and local securities by these three investment sources is laden with potential conflicts of interest. Municipal unions must sit across the bargaining table from state and local governments and demand wage increases, pension increments, and advantages in work rules. Their power is pronounced enough through their voting strength and potential for strikes and job actions, but to add to that power the ability to cut off loans to state and local governments, plunging them into bankruptcy, is to create a Frankenstein monster in local government. Casualty insurance companies must come to state government for approval of increases in premiums and for regulation on a wide range of issues including the financial soundness of the companies and their good faith in making insurance available to all drivers at reasonable rates. Savings banks and many savings and loan associations are chartered by state government and subject to state regulation over their ability to open branches, charge higher interest rates on mortgages, and make certain types of loans.

These bond purchases by insurance companies, savings banks, and pension funds pose a clear conflict of interest for state and local government. All three are, to one extent or another, regulated by state and local governments. If one day states and cities must come to insurance companies, savings banks, and municipal unions begging for loans and on the next day they are expected to control insurance premiums, regulate banking practices, and hold a tight rein on union wage demands, the conflict of interest becomes clear. As the New York fiscal crisis has unfolded the evidence of this conflict of interest has begun to accumulate. Its most obvious manifestation occurred when savings banks stepped forward to purchase large amounts of state and local bonds in New York. While commercial banks were decreasing their purchases of state and local bonds by 75 percent between 1971 and 1977, savings banks were increasing their purchases by 500 percent, from $200 million to $1 billion. At first glance it is hard to understand why savings banks embraced state and local bonds. Traditionally, they had shied away from such investments, since, as mutual savings banks, they are not taxed on corporate profits and, as such, the tax exemption afforded by local notes and bonds was of no use or value.

A possible reason for their willingness to buy state and local bonds, particularly in New York, became apparent later in 1975 when the savings banks mounted a massive lobbying campaign to obtain permission from the state legislature in New York to issue checking accounts as well as savings accounts at their banks. Previously restricted to savings accounts, savings banks were finding increasing difficulty in holding their depositors against the competitive onslaught of commercial banks which were allowed to offer both checking and savings accounts to their customers. Indeed, several commercial banks had launched vigorous advertising campaigns to win away savings bank customers with the slogan "one-stop banking," noting that commercial banks afforded the opportunity for customers to maintain both checking and savings accounts under one roof while savings banks could only offer savings accounts.

Alarmed by the drain on their customers, savings banks fought hard to get permission from the New York State Legislature to offer checking accounts to their savings account customers. Shortly after the savings bank purchases of state and local bonds began, New York Governor Hugh L. Carey announced that he was recommending that savings banks be given the right to offer their customers checking accounts, an authorization they had sought and been denied for years. Liberals in the legislature tried to require that savings banks invest in urban mortgages as a condition for being given the checking account privilege. The governor overrode their opposition and secured legislation giving savings banks checking accounts without any quid pro quo.

Shortly after the passage of the checking account bill, Governor Carey endorsed the notion that savings banks, now subject to a flat ceiling on interest rates for home mortgages in New York State, should be subject, instead, to a flexible interest rate, rising and falling as national interest rates varied. The governor's position was a verbatim reflection of the view advanced by the savings banks but resisted by previous administrations and legislatures. Under pressure from the governor, legislation for a flexible interest rate passed the Assembly in 1977 but was stalled in the New York State Senate. A flexible interest rate would have allowed savings banks to charge more interest on home mortgages than the 8½ percent currently permitted by New York State law. It remains a key item on the savings bank legislature agenda, an initiative stoutly opposed by most consumer groups in the state.

Was Governor Carey's advocacy of the two most important demands of the savings banks tied to the purchase of state bonds by these same savings banks? There is no proof, but the implication that the two could be linked is clear. Indeed, one Democratic New York legislative leader told me off the record that "the banks would never have gotten to first base on checking accounts or flexible interest mortgages except for the fact that the governor needed them to buy bonds."

Even more interesting is the close relationship that has emerged between New York City union leaders and New York City government in the aftermath of the purchase by city union-controlled pension funds of $3.1 billion of city bonds. At the height of the fiscal crisis, city union leaders approved a policy of massive purchase of city bonds by their union's pension funds becoming, at once, the city's bankers and its employees. One is given to wonder how successfully the city government can deal with union leaders when each knows that New York could never survive financially if the unions decided to stop buying city bonds and notes.

The decision of the insurance industry to buy huge amounts of city and state paper is also worth examining. Fire and casualty insurance companies began decreasing their purchases of municipal bonds in the early seventies, reducing their purchases from $4.4 billion in 1972 to $2.1 billion in 1975. But then the tables turned and these companies increased their purchases to $2.9 billion in 1976 and an expected $3.6 billion in 1977.[11] Insurance companies are, of course, closely regulated by state government. Their premiums must be approved by state departments of insurance, and the terms of their policies and coverage are subject to strict public control.

The period of 1976-77 has been one of almost unprecedented increases in insurance premiums, especially in New York State. Between 1975 and 1977, auto insurance premiums, for example, have risen in New York by an astonishing 70 percent,[12] one of the highest rates of increase in the nation. By contrast, in New Jersey where the Insurance Department has been more strict in permitting insurance premium increases, rates have increased much less rapidly during the same period. Why has New York been so liberal and New Jersey so strict in permitting insurance premium increases? Has the desperate need of New York for purchasers of bonds and the relatively less pressing need of New Jersey anything to do with it? Again, one can only conjecture. New Jersey's tough consumer-oriented insurance commissioner, James Sheeran, says, however, that "there is no question but that insurance companies are using their leverage with state and local governments to try to force premium increases. Where a state depends heavily on these companies for bond sales, it is hard to turn around and deny these companies rate increases."[13]

In a sense, the northeastern city resident is paying twice for the withdrawal of banks from the municipal bond market—once in the increased interest rates city governments and their taxpayers must pay for these bonds and once again in the relaxation of state and city regulation of savings banks, insurance companies, and unions.

In all, cities have had a hard time weathering the strike against them by commercial banks. The refusal of these institutions to buy the same share of the municipal bond market as they have absorbed historically ranks as a key reason for the staggering deficits and the precarious finances of our nation's largest cities. Whether banks withdrew out of concern for the shaky condition of city finances or whether they caused that shaky condition by their withdrawal is the sort of question that can never truly be answered. But one thing is clear: The commercial banks of this nation—which are publicly regulated and should serve in the public interest—have systematically turned their backs on the nation's northeastern cities and brought down upon those cities huge extra interest and debt costs by their action.

4.

WHO CREATES SLUMS?

"Can't we pass this bill without that goddamn ornament?" John W. Larsen, president of the Bowery Savings Bank screamed at me through the phone. Larsen was hoarse and mad as hell. As president of the nation's largest savings bank, with over $4 billion in assets, "no" was not exactly the word to which he was most accustomed. As the informal leader of New York State savings banks, Larsen had been charged with the task of persuading Assembly Democratic Speaker Stanley Steingut to support legislation granting savings banks the right to issue checking accounts. As we have seen, this privilege was a key part of the savings bank strategy to counter the commercial bank efforts to woo away customers from the savings institutions. It was their top legislative priority, and the banks reacted none too kindly when the liberal Democratic members of the Assembly joined with the black and Puerto Rican members in demanding an end to the savings bank policy of denying mortgage loans to applicants from poor or low-income neighborhoods. To assure that savings banks alter this policy, these assemblymen sought to attach an amendment to the bill granting savings banks checking accounts to require that 10 percent of the new financial commitments of these banks be set aside for mortgages in poor neighborhoods. This was the "ornament" Larsen was getting exercised about.

Steingut was passionately concerned about the denial of mortgage money to low-income neighborhoods—even his own district was affected—and had instructed me in 1975 to tell the savings banks that it was either a bill granting checking account privileges to savings banks *with* the 10 percent mortgage lending requirement, or no bill at all. I wasn't eager to confront Larsen on the phone, but I had worked closely with Steingut on the antimortgage discrimination issue and was determined to see it through. My hesitancy in talking with Larsen was compounded by the fact that I had worked for seven years at the Citizens Budget Commission, a civic watchdog organization for which I went to work after college and of which John W. Larsen had been president.

"Why should we be required to make these mortgage loans?" Larsen wanted to know. "Why should we bear the brunt of stopping a trend toward housing deterioration?"

"You act like I am asking you to make a donation to United Jewish Appeal," I countered. "All we are asking is that you reverse your bank's own arbitrary policy of refusing to make loans in much of New York City which is causing the deterioration in the first place."

"But many of these communities are in terrible shape. How can we go in and hope to turn them around?" Larsen persisted.

"But John, these are the same communities from which your deposits come. All we want is for you to lend money to the same people in mortgages from whom you receive it in deposits." It seemed like a reasonable point, but it only served to get Larsen madder.

The problem of mortgage lending discrimination has grown into the major urban housing issue in the past decade. Savings banks have traditionally been the prime source of mortgage financing for the communities in which they are located. Unlike commercial banks, which are over entire cities and states, savings banks and savings and loan associations are localized in certain parts of each city. Thus, in New York, the East New York Savings Bank and the Harlem Savings Bank are each intended to accept deposits from people in their neighborhoods and to supply mortgage capital, as needed, to these same areas.

Mortgage financing is the key to the success or failure of real estate in most cities. Owners of real property derive income from their buildings through their monthly collection of tenant rentals. When rental income exceeds total expenses, the owner realizes a profit which provides him with an incentive to continue to maintain and rent his property. But in recent years this equation has broken down. Expenses have mounted rapidly and tenants have been unable to keep pace in their rent checks with these rapid increases in expenses.

Heating oil costs, for example, have more than doubled since the 1973 OPEC oil price increase, driving up the costs of housing very rapidly. Real property taxes, in New York City, for example, increased by an average of 10 percent a year during the last decade, further inflating housing costs.[1] But while this inflation was taking place, tenant incomes were rising only very slowly, especially in the more depressed parts of New York and other cities. Indeed, while in 1970 New York City tenants paid 20% of their income in rent, in 1975 they were paying 25 percent.[2] All over New York and other cities, tenants were strained to the breaking point to meet the rapid increases in the expenses of operating their buildings. In some cities, such as New York, rent-control laws operated to keep down tenant rents in the face of these inflationary pressures, but despite these controls rents rose dramatically. The average New York family paid about half the rent in 1965 that it paid in 1975.[3]

Rents still could not keep pace with expenses, and the profit upon which owners relied as an incentive to operating their buildings all but vanished in most of New York and other cities. If an owner could not expect to make much money from his rents, he had to realize a profit somehow or else he would lose interest in his property and walk away from it, no longer bothering to maintain or manage it. The answer is mortgage financing. If an owner can be confident that in a few years he can sell his property to a new buyer, he knows that while he may not profit from the month-to-month cash flow of rental income, he will make money from his property when he sells it. But no owner can sell his building unless a bank is willing to step forward and lend the potential buyer a mortgage. More to the point, no buyer in his right mind would bid on a building unless he could be confident not only that he could get a mortgage *now* but that a mortgage would be available ten or twenty years *hence* when he wants to sell the building.

By securing a ready flow of mortgage money, owners would find it possible to subsist financially off the inherent value of their property—realized by selling it—even when the monthly cash flow afforded an inadequate profit.

But mortgage money was not forthcoming. Savings banks, the usual source of mortgages, refused to lend money to urban neighborhoods and adopted informal, unspoken policies of refusing to lend in certain communities. This policy, called redlining, involves drawing a red line around certain areas on a map. The message of the line is clear to any lending officer: No mortgage loans there.

When mortgages stopped, the last hope for housing preservation began to vanish. What could owners do? They could not increase rents further. New York City tenants are already paying one quarter of their income in rent, and a third of the city's population is paying more than 35 percent of their income—one dollar in three—in rent. Costs could not be reduced. Fuel costs for northeastern urban buildings are set in the Middle East by people hardly interested in the problems of inner-city real property in the United States. Local governments, hard pressed for cash, were not in a position to cut property taxes. Owners were forced up against the wall. There was no hope of realizing a profit on the monthly rental income they received, and banks had made it impossible to sell the property and realize a profit from the sales price by their refusal to grant mortgages to the potential buyers.

Owners did the one thing they could do: They abandoned their buildings, simply got up and walked away.

The impact of housing deterioration in the northeastern city is terrifying. Every two years in New York City, 18,000 to 20,000 housing units are abandoned, enough to fill the entire city of Camden, New Jersey; counted every four years, enough is lost to fill Mobile, Alabama! Entire blocks of the South Bronx, Bedford-Stuyvesant, and Brownsville sections of New York City are abandoned, resembling wartime Europe at its most devastated. It is impossible to pass through these areas without understanding the drama of the urban crisis. These abandoned buildings loom like tombstones to the dead neighborhoods that they once comprised, their addresses like epitaphs; the vandals and junkies who sleep in the deserted hallways waking only to prey upon the living are ghouls in a real nightmare.

But these ghost buildings mean more than the loss of part of a city's housing stock. They mean the loss of neighborhoods, of investment capital, and of tax sources, each particularly deadly to a city's well-being. A city really *is* its neighborhoods. Its residents come to see their immediate surrounding blocks as a kind of small town in which they live and to which they go for social life, for food, and for a sense of community. The destruction of neighborhoods symbolizes the collapse of a city to its residents far more graphically than any economic index or unbalanced budget.

But the collapse of urban housing has more than a social impact: It is a direct cause of the fiscal insolvency faced by American cities. Housing is the prime source of the revenue of a city. The property tax is the root and the basis of urban government financing. Look at the proportion of locally raised revenues in major American cities that comes from the property tax:

PERCENTAGE OF LOCALLY RAISED CITY TAX REVENUES DERIVED FROM PROPERTY TAXES[4]

City	*% of Tax Revenues from Property Taxation*
Atlanta	64
Baltimore	70
Boston	99
Chicago	58
Cleveland	42
Dallas	70
Detroit	56
Houston	62
Los Angeles	69
Minneapolis-St. Paul	87
New York	58
Pittsburgh	66
San Diego	50
San Francisco	66

Without the property tax, cities faced an enormous falloff in their revenues. But as urban housing failed, unable to make a profit from rents or obtain a mortgage, owners simply stopped paying their property taxes. In New York City alone, uncollected real property taxes soared in 1976 to over $300 million, about half of the budget deficit New York City faced in 1977. In fact, had that $300 million been available to New York City, thirty thousand workers need not have lost their jobs in the massive layoffs caused by the budget crisis that gripped New York after 1975.

But this erosion in local tax revenues had an even more significant impact on the ability of cities to survive. Under the terms of most city financing structures, the property tax is pledged, by the state constitution, as the guarantee for repayment of bonds and notes with which the city borrows money. In New York, for example, the State Constitution specifies that cities can borrow up to 10 percent of the value of property within their borders and that each year the property tax must be sufficient to repay all the debts that the city must pay off in that year. Bond and note buyers look to the property tax as their security that the loans they are making to a city through their purchase of bonds and notes will be repaid.

But when the city found itself unable to collect its property taxes, the security afforded by the property tax to note and bond holders suddenly became worth less and less. Potential lenders to cities looked around at the mass of abandoned buildings and uncollected taxes and asked whether this was, indeed, secure collateral for their loans. The deterioration of housing caused nonpayment of property taxes, which, in turn, created a larger budget deficit than need otherwise have occurred. But it also undermined investor confidence, helping to hasten the coming of the New York City fiscal crisis and the fiscal turmoil that gripped other cities throughout the United States. *At the root of the fiscal crisis lay a housing crisis.* And at the root of the housing crisis lay a mortgage lending strike by the savings banks.

With this background, liberal members of the New York State Assembly stood firm in their insistence that banks lend money to inner-city mortgages if they were to entertain any hope of passing a bill extending checking account privileges to savings banks. Indeed, proof of the refusal of savings banks to make mortgage loans in cities has mounted over the years. A study by the New York Public Interest Research Group revealed that of the savings banks located in Brooklyn, New York, none had invested more than 6 percent of its assets in its home borough.[5] More recently, a study by the New York State Department of Banking of mortgage lending by New York City savings banks proved that 65 percent of the mortgage loans of these banks are made outside of New York State.[6]

Owners in New York simply could not get mortgages. The effect on housing morale was devastating. One owner of a particularly seedy building in Crown Heights in Brooklyn underscored the impact of redlining to me when I interviewed him in 1974 in connection with my study of housing deterioration for the New York University Real Estate Institute. "Why should I make any repairs?" he told me in a thick foreign accent. "Nobody will notice, they won't lend me money, they won't buy my building, they take one look at the address and they run screaming. Why should I hire a plumber? What for? Would you?"

In a 1972 Louis Harris survey in Crown Heights, 55 percent of the owners of medium-sized buildings and 75 percent of the owners of large buildings cited capital appreciation—increase in real estate value—as a "very important" reason for their original purchase of an urban property. But the Harris study found that 81 percent of Crown Heights property owners felt that their buildings had proven a poor investment, and 91 percent traced this to the absence of mortgage money for resale or refinancing.[7]

Yet despite the evidence of the existence of redlining and the demonstration of its disastrous social impact, it became difficult to persuade the New York State Legislature to require savings banks to make mortgage investments in redlined neighborhoods in New York City. Always the demand that banks end their policy of redlining was met by the same retort from the banks: "How can you ask us to risk our depositor's money by investing it in neighborhoods that may well survive, but might not? How can we take that chance when there are lots of prudent investments throughout the nation that we can make?" For some, the compelling social justice of asking banks to lend money to the communities from which their own deposits sprang made overriding sense. But, especially in the Republican-controlled State Senate, it became impossible to overcome the bank argument that redlining was necessary to protect bank assets.

We lost and the savings banks were successful, in 1976, in passing legislation giving them the right to offer checking accounts without any provision about dealing with redlining or requiring that mortgages be given in low-income areas. The defeat was largely due to the effectiveness of the savings banks' argument that it was unjust for them to assume the risks of such loans entirely on their own shoulders.

This reversal stimulated me to try to understand how mortgages could be generated in poor neighborhoods without running afoul of the savings bank objections about the excessive risks of such loans. Naturally, my attention was drawn to the Federal Housing Administration (FHA), the mechanism that was established in 1934 under the National Housing Act to insure mortgage loans. FHA should be the full answer to the savings bank objections about assuming the risk of poor neighborhood mortgage lending. Established in the aftermath of the Great Depression, FHA was conceived as a method of stimulating mortgage flow to housing even amid financial insecurity about the prospect for repayment.

During the Great Depression, housing construction and resale ground virtually to a standstill as worried banks denied mortgage loans for fear that the sagging economy could offer no realistic prospect that the mortgages could ever be repaid. Foreclosures abounded as more and more homeowners fell behind in their payments to savings banks, further traumatizing these institutions and encouraging them to turn off the spigot on mortgage lending. But the nation needed housing and demanded that mortgages continue to flow. Savings institutions made the argument they later repeated to the New York Legislature when the redlining issue was raised: How can we risk our depositor's money on shaky mortgage loans?

The FHA was the answer, a government program of loan insurance to guarantee mortgages and thus persuade timid savings banks and other mortgage lenders to make these loans so vitally needed by the economy. The concept of FHA was simple: Spread the risk of mortgages over the entire population through a government guarantee and finance the insurance program through a mortgage insurance premium of one quarter or one half of 1 percent added onto the price of every insured mortgage. This mortgage insurance premium created a fund sufficient to absorb any losses caused by bad mortgage loans and permitted the federal government to rekindle enough bank confidence to start up again the flow of mortgages.

Ever since the Depression, the motivating concept behind FHA remained that the government stood ready to insure mortgages that might otherwise be too risky for a bank to undertake without insurance. But FHA changed in 1969 when Richard M. Nixon became President and the vaunted "southern strategy" became the political law of the land. In a rush to gratify the needs of southern conservative constituents and to lure them away from George Wallace, the Californian President set about to change the purpose and role of the FHA. No longer was it an agency designed to shore up bank confidence in areas suffering from a shortage of mortgage capital. FHA became, instead, a mechanism to direct bank investment *away* from northeastern cities and toward the booming Sun Belt. No longer were mortgages insured in the inner city or in the Northeast; instead the bulk of FHA insurance commitments flowed south where it acted to attract mortgage money from all over the nation with the lure of a building boom supplemented by the attractions of federal insurance.

In 1975, for example, the states of Florida, California, and Arizona—the heartland of the Sun Belt boom—attracted 29 percent of FHA's mortgage insurance commitments while having only 15 percent of the nation's population. New York City, by contrast, with 3.6 percent of America's people, got only 2.1 percent of FHA's mortgage commitments. A Sun Belt bias became all too evident in the FHA. The fifteen states of the Sun Belt, with 38 percent of America's people, got 49 percent of FHA's mortgage insurance while the fifteen states of the Northeast, with 45 percent of the population, received only 33 percent of FHA mortgage insurance.

FEDERAL HOUSING ADMINISTRATION MORTGAGE INSURANCE, 1975[8]

Northeast			Sun Belt		
State	*% U.S. Pop.*	*% Total Mortgages Insured*	*State*	*% U.S. Pop.*	*% Total Mortgages Insured*
Connecticut	1.5	.8	Alabama	1.7	1.9
Illinois	5.4	5.0	Arizona	1.0	3.7

State	*% U.S. Pop.*	*% Total Mortgages Insured*	*State*	*% U.S. Pop.*	*% Total Mortgages Insured*
Indiana	2.5	1.6	Arkansas	1.0	.6
Maine	0.5	0.2	California	9.8	18.1
Massachusetts	2.8	.9	Florida	3.7	6.9
Michigan	4.3	4.4	Georgia	2.3	2.0
Minnesota	1.2	4.1	Louisiana	1.8	1.2
New Hampshire	.4	.6	Mississippi	1.1	.9
New Jersey	3.5	3.0	New Mexico	.5	.6
New York	8.7	4.7	North Carolina	2.5	1.5
Ohio	5.1	3.6	Oklahoma	1.3	1.7
Pennsylvania	5.7	2.7	South Carolina	1.3	.9
Rhode Island	.5	.2	Tennessee	2.0	1.6
Vermont	.2	.1	Texas	5.6	5.7
Wisconsin	2.2	.8	Virginia	2.3	1.4
TOTAL	44.5	32.7	TOTAL	37.9	48.7

The FHA thus does the exact opposite of what it was intended to do. Instead of fueling mortgage lending in deteriorating areas in need of a shot in the arm, it encourages lending in areas already glutted with new construction, building, and expansion, draining away mortgages from areas that need them. If a New York banker is reluctant to lend his money in Brooklyn as opposed to Florida because the Brooklyn economy is on the skids and the Florida growth boom in full swing, think of the impact on his decision if he knows that he can get federal insurance in Florida but not in Brooklyn!

FHA argues that, in favoring the Sun Belt, it is merely following the national trend toward mortgages in the South. One FHA official told me, "All we are doing is providing insurance where the mortgages are." But that is just the point. FHA is not supposed to *follow* the market, it is supposed to *lead* it. It is supposed to answer the question asked by the savings banks: "Why are we being asked to risk our depositor's money in making mortgages in areas that are needy?" With FHA the nation as a whole assumes the risk, not just a few bankers. But FHA has been nowhere to be found.

I shared this data with Donald Ross, executive director of the New York Public Interest Research Group, whose study of the redlining issue first helped bring the problem to broad public attention. He said, "It's strange but you never hear about the FHA or its role. You can talk about redlining anywhere and you just don't hear about how the federal government may be behind redlining with its insurance policies."

FHA's influence on mortgage investment is silent, unpublicized, uncriticized, and deadly. It imparts a federal stamp of approval to redlining and permits a banker to say to his critics that he is not exercising social judgment in lending money in the South; he is merely lending where he has a chance to get loan insurance.

The federal impact on urban housing did not stop with the FHA, however. The Nixon administration engineered an about-face in federal construction policies, denying funds to the Northeast while subsidizing construction in other parts of the nation. The tax base of the northeastern city eroded in the face of this policy beyond all projections and brought the cities face to face with fiscal disaster. During the late sixties and early seventies, a building boom had sustained the economies of many northeastern cities—New York in particular. New office buildings, massive rehabilitation programs, publicly subsidized middle-income housing, and public housing for the poor not only improved the living conditions of New Yorkers but added vital dollars to the base of real property upon which the city depended for its tax revenues. Between 1965 and 1975, the assessed value of real property in New York City rose from $32 billion to $40 billion, an astonishingly rapid rate of increase.[9] The increment meant that the property tax revenues of New York City climbed from $1.6 billion in 1965 to $3.1 billion in 1975.[10] Much of the spending of the Lindsay years in New York was defrayed by the building boom and the property taxes it threw off.

The building boom meant that cities could borrow more. Their expanding base of real property strengthened investor confidence in the city's financial solidity and its future. Since the debt limit—the legal maximum the New York State Constitution permits its cities to borrow—is tied to the amount of property in the city, the growth in construction meant that the city's borrowing could continue and even accelerate.

But the boom stopped in the mid-seventies. Between 1975 and 1977, the assessed evaluation of city real property has remained almost unchanged from $40 billion to $40.5 billion.[11] The boom is over. Unemployment in the construction industry is variously reported at over 20 percent, and a death rattle has gripped office building construction in the Big Apple.

But this slack in construction is not unique to New York. It is the product of a deliberate mix of federal policies to foster rural and suburban housing at the expense of urban construction. Between 1972 and 1975, the northeastern states, with 52 percent of America's population, were the locus of only 35 percent of its new housing construction. When housing was built, it was not in the city, but in the surrounding area. Between 1971 and 1975, the percent of new housing construction in center cities had fallen from 29 percent to 21 percent while the proportion in rural areas had climbed from 17 percent to 26 percent.[12]

The federal government lay squarely behind this falloff in construction in the Northeast. FHA insurance, a key element in obtaining mortgage financing for new construction, was increasingly denied the northeastern city, as we have seen. Without FHA insurance, builders and developers found it more difficult than ever to obtain mortgages.

Federal subsidies to housing construction were cut sharply under Nixon and Ford. Initially, subsidization under federal housing programs was frozen by Nixon and, even when unfrozen by Ford, was very slow in coming. But the real death knell for housing in America's cities was sounded by the commercial banks. The shortage of mortgage money that arose from the policy of savings banks of redlining urban neighborhoods was alleviated, throughout the fifties and sixties, by mortgage loans made by state and local governments. Acting as a bank, state and local governments acted to supplement the meager flow of funds from private banks with their own loan programs. The housing projects that dot urban skylines throughout the nation were mostly built with government, not private, mortgages. These mortgages were lent by public agencies to private developers who, in turn, agreed to accept certain profit limitations and to repay the mortgage loans through the proceeds of the rentals they collected from the properties. The funds for these mortgages were raised by state and local governments through the sale of bonds and notes to banks and the investing public. These states and localities, in turn, pledged to use the money paid them by the project's owners to repay the bonds and notes upon which the mortgages were based.

State and local governments pledged to support the bonds in the event rentals proved inadequate to repay them through direct tax appropriations. In some cases, these commitments were legally binding upon state and local governments, but in others they were only "moral obligations" not embodied in law or approved by popular referendum. When banks stopped buying state and local bonds, housing bonds were an early casualty. If banks and the investing public were reluctant to buy bonds whose security was guaranteed in the state and federal constitutions, they were certainly unwilling to buy bonds backed only by the "moral obligation" of the state and local government.

Without housing bond revenues, the state and local governments of the Northeast found themselves without funds to finance new housing construction. Private mortgages were unavailable from banks, which continued to turn their backs on the housing needs of the cities and states from which they drew their deposits. FHA was unwilling to insure mortgages in the urban Northeast, since it did not fit in with the Mitchell-Nixon-Ford southern strategy. And now even public mortgages could not be given, since commercial banks and other investors shied away from housing bonds backed only by a "moral obligation."

A congressional remedy seemed in the making in 1974 when the United States Congress passed the Housing and Community Development Act. In Section 802 of that act there was a provision dealing with just this problem, authorizing the federal Department of Housing and Urban Development to guarantee bonds issued for housing by states and cities. The provision called for federal backing for taxable state and local bonds and a federal subsidy to cover the difference in interest rate the locality had to bear because the bonds would be taxable as opposed to tax-exempt, the more usual form of state and local financing.

The provision was a godsend. It would make possible a major infusion of mortgage money into urban areas. Bonds for housing would now be salable—because of their federal backing—and the funds they raised could be pumped by willing state and local governments into needy urban communities. There was one problem: The Ford administration adamantly refused to implement the program. Although the program had been established by a federal law signed by the President, the Department of Housing and Urban Development refused to make any guarantees or to request any appropriation for the subsidy.

So housing construction in American northeastern cities stopped, the growth in the real estate tax base of these communities was halted, and the process of deterioration speeded. Examining the fiscal crisis of the American city is like peeling an onion. First you have the fiscal crisis, a shortage of tax revenues, and an inability to borrow except at inflated interest rates. Then beneath lingers a housing crisis, cutting into property tax revenues and undermining investor confidence in the security of city bonds and notes. Still further beneath lies the refusal of the federal government to insure northeastern mortgages or to back northeastern housing bonds.

Indeed, as the past four chapters indicate, the fiscal crisis of the American city is really only marginally of its own making. Eliminate the excessive payments to welfare landlords, social service administrators, Medicaid doctors, nursing homes, Medicaid mills, and hospitals; eliminate the high interest rates states and cities must pay for their bonds and notes and restore to them access to commercial bank funds—do these and you have virtually eliminated the deficit in the budgets of states and cities. Restore mortgage financing and government mortgage insurance to urban real property and you have bolstered tax revenues in most cities sufficiently to provide a surplus. But as long as profiteering off public welfare programs persists and commercial banks continue to boycott urban bonds and notes while savings banks refuse to lend urban mortgages, then a fiscal crisis will persist, dramatically, drastically, and probably incurably.

In these previous four chapters, we have explored the real villains of the urban fiscal crisis. They turn out not to be liberals or the poor but rather those who profiteer off welfare and Medicaid and those who refuse to lend money to cities on their housing and the federal policies that support their refusal. In the remainder of this book, we will explore the causes of the crisis that lies beneath the fiscal crisis—the economic crisis that grips the American city, a crisis characterized by an unemployment and inflation rate well above the national average and a rate of growth well below it.

The preconditions of this urban economic crisis relate to the higher cost of living in northeastern cities as opposed to that which prevails in the rest of America. This cost-of-living gap sets in motion a chain reaction of economic circumstance that dooms the Northeast to greater and greater poverty and less potential for economic expansion.

We often tend to misunderstand the depth of the imbalance in costs of living throughout the United States. But the gap is so huge and so wide that it creates a totally different economic environment in one part of the nation—the rural, the southern, and the western—than in the other part—the northeastern, the Great Lakes area, and the urban. According to the Bureau of Labor Statistics of the United States Government, a living standard that costs $29,677 in New York City and costs $29,187 in Boston costs only $21,410 in Atlanta and $21,482 in Houston. It is instructive to compare costs of living for an upper-middle-income family in different American cities to understand how enormous the gap in living costs has really become.

HIGHER INCOME LIVING COSTS IN SELECTED CITIES[13]

Northeast		Sun Belt	
City	*Living Cost*	*City*	*Living Cost*
New York	$29,677	Houston	$21,482
Boston	29,187	Atlanta	21,410
Minneapolis	24,556	Dallas	21,393
Detroit	24,226	Southwest rural	20,606
Chicago	23,804	Southern rural	19,442

These higher living costs result from a variety of factors. Underlying them, however, are two key elements: energy and food. the higher utility costs, housing rental charges, and basic living expenses of the urban northeastern family are rooted in these two essential commodities. The impact of these higher living costs is pivotal. They mean that it costs more to live in the Northeast, to do business there, to locate a factory there, or to run a government. But what causes higher energy and food prices? In the next two chapters, the answer emerges: deliberate and systematic federal policies.

5. THE ENERGY WINDFALL

In December of 1973, I flew from New York to Dallas, Texas. On my way out to New York's La Guardia Airport, I stopped for gas and had to wait for almost an hour in line to fill my tank. I was furious and almost missed my plane. Cars were backed up for blocks, creeping forward inch by inch to their place in the sun by the gas pump. When I got to Texas, my friend rented a car and we drove away from the airport. En route to Dallas, we stopped for gas and drove right up to the pump, no problems, no wait. I was incredulous at the difference between my experience in New York and in the South. At the gas station, I mentioned to the attendant the problems I had in getting gas earlier in the day in New York.

"I've been reading about those gas lines up North," he drawled. "They must really be something." There really seemed to be no energy crisis in the South, although the rest of the nation was strangling for want of fuel. When the price increases came and the energy supplies again began to flow, I was reminded on every trip to the South of the fact that energy prices in the Northeast were out of all proportion to those in the Sun Belt South.

There are really two separate energy crises. One is the shortage of energy, which endangers the future of our entire country. But the other crisis is the growing gap in energy prices among areas of the nation. This gap, more than any other single factor, has impelled a vast transfer of wealth from the Northeast to the Sun Belt. The overall national energy crisis has stirred vast national concern. From President Carter down to the local level, government planners are worried about the looming shortage of energy while economists ponder the prospect of rapidly inflating energy costs reflective of this basic scarcity. But very little attention has been given the crisis of *different* costs in different parts of America. Since energy costs are basic to housing, transportation, utility, and other expenses, major differences in energy costs among regions of America create radically varied economic circumstances. The twentieth-century mobility of people, businesses, and capital translates these differences in energy cost levels into a massive migration to the South and the Sun Belt and away from the Northeast. All the efforts of the national administration to deal with the energy crisis go to the dual questions of energy scarcity and energy inflation, but few of them deal with the problems of differences in energy costs in different regions of America.

The energy price variation arises partially because the Northeast must use imported oil as opposed to oil that is produced domestically. While the United States as a whole imports only 7.8 million barrels of oil daily and generates the remaining 9.9 million barrels it uses domestically, the Northeast must import 90 percent of the oil it uses.[1] Of course, this necessity for importation arises from the fact that no oil is produced in the Northeast and that this nation's great oil reserves lie in the Sun Belt states. The Alaskan oil, now flowing through a pipeline to the continental United States, is used largely in the West, further decreasing the dependence of the rest of America on imported petroleum. This reliance on imported oil in the Northeast is not new, but two factors have combined to increase its importance. In the first place, national energy consumption has risen rapidly so that the nation's domestic oil reserves have become increasingly inadequate to supply America's energy needs. As domestic oil has come to provide a lesser share of America's oil needs, the amount of oil available for sale to the Northeast has dropped sharply. There is not enough domestic oil to go around, and the regions closer to the oil wells are using more of it for their own needs and sending less to the Northeast.

But, more importantly, the Northeast's need to import oil has become more expensive. Prior to the 1973 decision of the oil-producing (OPEC) nations to increase their oil prices, imported and domestically produced oil were basically priced at similar levels. But the OPEC decision changed things dramatically. While the domestic oil price remained fixed by federal regulation at $8.94 per barrel, the OPEC nations charged $14.69 per barrel and increase their price almost annually.[2] Thus, the Northeast must buy its oil in a *world* energy market controlled by Arab and other foreign interests who are free to peg petroleum prices at any level. But the rest of America buys its oil from a domestic market, rigidly regulated by the Congress and wholly under the jurisdiction of federal laws.

In 1974, after a year of gap between imported and domestic oil prices, the entitlements program was established to equalize costs between the two types of oil. The system requires that domestic oil refiners pay a subsidy to imported oil refiners to equalize the price of the two. But the federal regulation only applies to imported oil that is refined *in* the United States (some 1.9 billion barrels), not the 800 million barrels of foreign oil that are refined abroad and imported into the United States only as refined products. For these barrels, mainly used in the Northeast, the difference in prices continue. The net result is a dramatically higher price for oil in the Northeast which, in turn, drives up home heating, industrial fuel, utility, and transportation costs. For example, home heating oil that would cost $2 in New England costs about $.60 in the South.[3] Similarly, 500 kilowatts of electricity in New York City costs $37, but the same amount of power in Houston costs only $15. Look at the vast differences in energy prices between northeastern and Sun Belt cities:

COST OF 500 KILOWATT HOURS OF ELECTRICITY[4]

Northeast		Sun Belt	
City	*Cost*	*City*	*Cost*
New York	$37.33	Los Angeles	$19.91
Boston	24.86	San Diego	18.79
Philadelphia	24.82	Atlanta	17.57
Pittsburgh	22.50	Dallas	17.44
Detroit	21.26	Houston	15.02

Not only does the Northeast use more expensive oil, but it uses *more* oil as opposed to lower-priced fuels such as coal and natural gas. Right after the 1977 New York City power blackout, I went to North Carolina to work on a political campaign. At a seemingly interminable political dinner I was obliged to attend, I sat next to a member of the North Carolina Public Utilities Commission. We talked about the New York blackout and what might have been its cause and I asked him what kind of fuel North Carolina utilities used to generate electricity. He answered that the state's utilities used about 30 percent nuclear power, about 65 percent coal, and only about 2 percent oil. "Oil is just too expensive," he added. I nodded agreement and told him that in New York City we had to use about 85 percent oil, 15 percent nuclear, and no coal at all to provide our electricity. "That's why it's so expensive up there," the commissioner concluded.

In the northeastern city, we cannot burn coal unless we choose not to breathe clean air. The pollution that would result from coal burning is just not an acceptable price to pay for low utility bills in the northeastern city. Indeed, not only must New York utilities refrain from burning coal, but they must use only low sulfur oil, an especially expensive fuel reduced in sulfur content to minimize the amount of sulfur dioxide pumped into the atmosphere when it is burned. Low sulfur fuel is a necessity in a city as crowded as New York, but it adds substantially to the cost of energy. Thus, the Consolidated Edison Company, serving New York City, must pay $.87 for the same amount of power-generating heat that costs only $.55 in upstate New York.[5] The difference arises from the fact that Con Edison must burn low sulfur oil, whereas upstate utilities, in nonurban locations, can burn coal and high sulfur oil.

The Northeast is also unique for its lesser use of natural gas, a fuel that is a mainstay of energy supply in the rest of the nation, but only a more minor part of the northeastern energy demand. Natural gas prices are regulated by the Congress and are now only gradually being deregulated under the Carter energy program. Because natural gas prices are regulated and imported oil prices are basically not (set by the OPEC cartel, not by congressional action), the Northeast is in the position of using a fuel that is more expensive—oil—while the rest of America uses natural gas, which is set at a lower price by congressional action. The Federal Power Commission estimated, in 1976, that natural gas in America costs about $4 to $5 for the same amount of energy as cost $12 when supplied by oil.

Of course, the rest of America can use natural gas while the Northeast must use oil because of geography: The natural gas comes from southern and western states and they cream off the bulk of the supply for their own use, leaving very little for "export" to the Northeast. The Northeast is thus in the same position as Western Europe—dependent on the exports of energy producing regions of the world—while the Sun Belt and the South enjoy the favored position of an oil producing region, our own domestic OPEC.

But much of the price difference between the Sun Belt and the Northeast is created, oddly enough, by the misguided actions of our own northeastern members of Congress. This problem was first brought to my attention by Governor Thomas P. Salmon of Vermont, with whom I worked in his unsuccessful bid for the United States Senate. During a mock question-and-answer session to prepare him for a debate against his Republican opponent, I asked him whether he supported the deregulation of natural gas. This question, long a litmus test of proconsumer as opposed to proindustry politicians, would matter a great deal to the liberal Vermont electorate and I expected to hear the pro forma, liberal answer about the need for government regulation to protect the consumer from unwarranted energy price increases. I was very surprised at the answer I got. A tough-spoken, bright, but seasoned politician, Salmon jammed the question down my throat. "I am sick and tired of hearing the standard liberal answer to that question. Liberals always say they are for regulation to keep down natural gas prices. But they don't stop to realize that natural gas is far more heavily used in the Sun Belt and the Midwest than in the Northeast. The Northeast uses much more oil. Imported oil is not regulated—certainly not in any way the OPEC cartel will recognize. We in the Northeast have to pay through the nose for oil, while the rest of the nation sits by and uses price-controlled natural gas. I think we had better start looking at that disparity and consider how to equalize the price they pay for regulated natural gas and the price we pay for unregulated oil."

The Salmon view was an entirely new perspective to me. Like many liberals, I had seen issues like regulation on a business versus consumer basis. I had seen the issue in very simplistic terms and had never really looked at the consequences of different regulatory policies over different energy sources used by different parts of the country. That is not, of course, to say that natural gas prices should just be raised, but rather that they should be adjusted as part of an overall plan to equalize national energy costs. The debate over deregulation of natural gas has posed the interesting spectacle of liberal northeastern members of Congress arguing for price controls and Sun Belt legislators, responsive to the demands of the gas producers, arguing for deregulation—each staunchly clinging to a point of view designed to harm their own constituents. I suppose there is a lesson in the fact that Salmon was defeated in his race for the Senate.

Throughout this review of the reasons for energy price differences in regions of the nation emerges one basic fact: The federal government has chosen to take a "hands-off" policy where regional differences in energy prices are concerned. It is quite willing to permit the proximity of the Sun Belt to oil and natural gas wells to militate for lower energy prices there while allowing the Northeast to pay more for its fuel. The entire benefit of domestic fuel production inures to one section of the nation and the entire burden of importation rests on another part. Nor does the federal government consider any action to defray the extra energy costs imposed on the Northeast by its inability to burn coal or higher sulfur fuel because of the likely air pollution consequences. The federal government's laissez-faire attitude dooms the Northeast to perpetually higher energy costs than are borne by the rest of the nation. The result is that transportation, heating, housing, industrial production, electricity, and virtually everything else cost more in the Northeast and less in the Sun Belt. This difference in the cost of living sets up preconditions for residence or business in the Northeast that puts the region at a gross competitive disadvantage with the rest of the nation.

The energy crisis has raised fuel prices all over the nation, but it has raised them dramatically more in the Northeast than in the Sun Belt. In the process, it has created an energy bonanza for the South and the West. It becomes cheaper to do business in the South, less expensive to locate a factory or a corporate headquarters there, and, above all, substantially cheaper to live there.

Actually, there is no logical reason—other than the accident of geography—for the Northeast to pay more for its oil. The fact is that the northeastern city is highly efficient in its use of power, its density providing a shield against excessive energy utilization. As the following chart demonstrates, energy use in the Northeast lags substantially below the per capita national average.

ENERGY USE AS PERCENT OF NATIONAL AVERAGE[6]

State	*Per Capita Energy Use (% of national average)*
Texas	177
New Mexico	172
Alabama	125
Ohio	108
Massachusetts	77
Connecticut	75
New York	71
Rhode Island	63

It is interesting to note, for example, that the state of North Carolina, with about 5 million people, uses a maximum of about 11,500 megawatts of electric power while New York City, with 8 million, uses a peak of only about 8,500 megawatts. Were energy prices to bear any relationship to energy use patterns, one could be pardoned for jumping to the conclusion that northeastern energy costs should be lower than those in the rest of America rather than markedly higher.

But the higher energy prices paid in the Northeast and the drain of jobs, population, and capital to the Sun Belt that it causes is only half of the story. Ultimately, a situation is created by the dynamics of the international energy trade in which the oil dollars paid by the Northeast themselves end up in the pockets of Sun Belt businessmen. The Northeast may pay for its oil and give its money to the Arabs, but it is the Sun Belt regions of America that are the ultimate repository for these oil dollars.

During 1975, I was first aware of this trend when I noticed news reports of a huge increase in American exports abroad. In 1972, before the Arab oil price increase, American exports to the rest of the world totaled $50 billion, or 4.3 percent of our gross national product. But by 1975 American exports had more than doubled to $108 billion, or 7.1

percent of our gross national product.[7] So rapid a growth caught my eye and I investigated further to determine the source of the rapid increase in exports. On closer examination, it appeared that exports to OPEC (oil-producing) nations accounted for much of this increase. In 1972 American exports to OPEC nations totaled only $3 billion, but in 1975 they ran up to $13 billion, over four times as much. Exports to Near East countries, excluding Israel, had risen from $1.4 billion in 1972 to $7.4 billion in 1975.[8]

It was clear that the United States, sapped of much of its wealth by the high price of the oil it imported, was getting back much of this money through increased export sales to oil-producing nations. Of course, the oil-producing nations were also investing their wealth in the United States, purchasing real property and interests in American businesses. But these *investments* were designed to produce a profit for the OPEC nations. When OPEC countries bought American products, it was an outright return of dollars to the American economy, quite distinguishable from investments.

If our oil dollars were flowing back to us as a nation through export sales to OPEC nations, the key question loomed: From whom was the oil money being taken by OPEC and to whom was it being returned when American products were bought? The first question has an obvious answer. The Northeast accounts for the vast bulk of American oil imports and it is from the northeasterner that the bill for imported oil is paid. Every time Arab oil flows into northeastern cars, utility boilers, or home heating units, the citizens of the states from Maine to Pennsylvania were paying the bill for oil imports.

But once the Arabs got the money for their oil, if they then used much of it to buy American products, whose products were they buying and who profited from the purchases? To answer this question, it was necessary to examine closely the mix of American exports to the rest of the world and to pinpoint which commodities had increased most rapidly in their export volume. I came up with the following list:[9]

SELECTED AMERICAN EXPORTS, 1972-1975

Export Commodity	*1972 (in billions)*	*1975 (in billions)*
Food and live animals	$5.7	$17.0
Motor vehicles (military and civilian)	4.5	10.7
Aircraft (military and civilian)	3.0	7.0
Construction and mining equipment	under 1.0	6.9
Power generating equipment	1.8	4.0
Coal	1.0	3.9
TOTAL	16.2	49.5

It is interesting that none of these commodities is made in significant quantity in any of the northeastern states—New England, New York, New Jersey, and Pennsylvania—except for some in the industrial areas of Pennsylvania. Two of the fastest growing exports—food and coal—are, of course, completely nonnortheastern in nature, and the industrial commodities—largely of a military nature—are heavily concentrated in Sun Belt defense plants. Particularly in dealings with the OPEC nations, arms played an increasingly large role in American export trade, and the American aerospace and military industrial complex is primarily located in the Sun Belt South, as we will explore in Chapter 10.

Thus, the pattern is quite clear. Northeastern oil dollars are flowing abroad for the purchase of high-price fuel and are then returned to America through sale abroad of commodities made elsewhere in the nation. The energy crisis lays the basis for a massive transfer of wealth out of the Northeast to the OPEC nations and back again to the Sun Belt South.

The energy crisis thus represented a double bonanza for the Sun Belt: on the one hand, a lower energy price with which to attract northern jobs, capital, and people and, on the other hand, access to OPEC countries to sell their products and thus reap back the oil dollars paid by the beleaguered northeastern oil customers.

But what was it that permitted the South to reap the benefits of increased sales to OPEC while the North did not? Much of the answer lies in the fact that OPEC nations needed, preeminently, two types of American products—food and arms. Food is, of course, not a northeastern product by the dictates of geography and population density. The arms trade is a southern-dominated field because of the bias of the national defense budget in favor of the Sun Belt and against the Northeast. We will explore later how this bias developed and how massive is its extent, but it is worth noting here that there is no natural reason why the Sun Belt should be given the preponderance of federal defense contracts other than the more skillful lobbying of the southern members of Congress over the past three decades. For years, this southern advantage in defense industries has led to a drain of wealth from the Northeast to the Sun Belt, but when domestic arms consumption is considered alongside of the demands of the foreign arms trade, the southern domination of defense industry has enabled the Sun Belt to get an advantage in competing for northeastern oil dollars as well.

In all, the federal view of the energy crisis has been uniquely and perhaps deliberately myopic when it has come to understanding how this national crisis affects the Northeast in particular. Consider the failures of federal policy to take account of the fact that:

- the northeastern cities cannot burn coal, America's cheapest fuel, because of the air pollution that would inevitably result. (It is worth noting that strictures against urban coal burning result, in part, from congressionally set national air quality standards embodied in the Clean Air Act.)
- the Northeast does not have equal access to domestically produced oil, an accident of geography transformed by OPEC pricing policies, into an economic disaster of monumental proportions.
- similarly, the Northeast has only limited access to natural gas, most of which is used by regions closer to the sources of production.
- not only must the Northeast burn imported oil, but it must burn the most expensive imported oil—low sulfur fuel—in many of its cities to decrease air pollution.
- and, finally, the Northeast cannot recapture its lost oil dollars through international trade, since it does

> not produce food and since it has not been the beneficiary of federal defense contracts to develop a local arms industry.

American negotiators argued at the 1976 world economic summit conference between rich and developing nations that proximity to natural resources and raw materials does not confer upon a nation the right to hold the industrialized world hostage or to force it to pay exorbitant prices for its fuel or resources. American foreign policy spokesmen have said for years that the Arabs are shortsighted in throwing the world into recession and depression by manipulation of energy prices and the use of the leverage afforded them by their oil production to reap huge profits.

These exact arguments should be applied domestically. The proximity of the Sun Belt to oil and gas must not give it a license to drain away wealth from the Northeast through the creation of a two-tiered energy pricing system in the United States—one for the Sun Belt using coal, natural gas, and domestic oil and another for the Northeast using imported oil. If it is shortsighted for the Arabs to trigger a depression in industrialized countries by forcing on them a higher energy price, it is equally shortsighted for the Sun Belt to trigger a regional depression in the Northeast by making it pay more for energy.

The Northeast needs federal action to average energy costs throughout the nation. The higher price of foreign oil is caused, not by the Northeast's action, but by national and international policies and cartels. It is unfair for one region of America to bear the brunt of the failures of American foreign policy to contain the prices of imported raw materials and fuels. The shortage of energy, which lies behind the higher power prices, is actually far more the fault of the Sun Belt than of the Northeast. Cities conserve energy while the lower density of the Sun Belt areas uses vastly more than its share. When the energy needs of 5 million North Carolinians are almost 50 percent greater than those of 8 million New Yorkers, one cannot lay the energy shortage at the doorstep of the Northeast.

The federal government must recognize that internal differences in energy prices cannot be tolerated. The special needs of each region of the nation should be recognized and borne by all other regions so that we have one price for energy throughout the United States. To continue the current wide variations is to doom certain regions to economic disaster and to encourage in others runaway economic growth, both perils to our national growth and stability.

6.

THE SUPERMARKET SWINDLE

I felt like it was the best supermarket sale I had ever encountered. White bread, usually $.44 a loaf was only $.32. Hamburger meat was only $.82 a pound, not the $1.12 I had been used to paying. Chicken, which usually cost me $.65 a pound in New York, cost only $.48. But it was no special sale. There were no huge posters proclaiming heroic bargains and the customers were not flocking to cram their carts full of food while the specials lasted. In fact, the prices weren't special at all; they were just the normal food prices one paid in Dallas, Texas, on that September afternoon in 1976.

While in Dallas, I had decided to make a detour to the supermarket to compare food prices with those I had recorded at my neighborhood A&P in New York before I left. The results brought home to me more clearly than any consumer price index ever could the vast disparity in food prices between the North and the South. Compare the basic staples in my market basket in each city:

SELECTED NEW YORK AND DALLAS FOOD PRICES COMPARED, 1976

Commodity	*New York*	*Dallas*
Loaf of white bread	$ .44	$ .32
Sirloin steak (per lb.)	2.14	1.79
Hamburger (per lb.)	1.12	.82
Chicken	.65	.48
Milk	.43	.43
Eggs (doz.)	.97	.88
TOTAL	$5.75	$4.73

But the shoppers in Dallas did not seem to regard the prices as low. When I commented on how cheap bread was, an elderly woman turned to me and said, in her deep southern drawl, "You must be from up North, why just last month, the bread here was two cents less." The federal data confirms that we have two distinct and separate schedules of food prices in America—the northern and the southern. According to the federal Bureau of Labor Statistics food that costs $4,500 in Dallas costs $5,600 in New York City.[1]

These differences are not minor, nor can they be easily explained by geographic locations. Certainly, meat should be cheaper in Dallas than in New York but why should it be cheaper throughout the South than it is throughout the North? Why should butter and other dairy products cost more in the North despite the concentration of dairy farmers in the Northeast and the Northeast's proximity to the great midwestern dairy regions?

I was also surprised to note that food prices have been increasing more rapidly in the Northeast than they have in the rest of the country. It is interesting to compare the rate of price increase in the basic commodities in New York and Philadelphia with that in Atlanta and Dallas. (This data reflects price increases between 1967 and 1976 in New York and

Philadelphia on the one hand and Dallas and Atlanta on the other, as recorded by the Consumer Price Index in each city.)

FOOD INFLATION IN NEW YORK-PHILADELPHIA AND ATLANTA-DALLAS, 1967-1976[2]

Commodity	*% Increase in the North*	*% Increase in the South*
White bread	67	55
Steak	74	57
Chicken	64	58
Butter	60	43
Eggs	91	78
Coffee	167	133

This disparity in food prices creates an underlying impetus toward a higher living cost in the North than in the South. Later in the book, we will examine the economic consequences of this cost-of-living disparity, but it is, nonetheless, significant that it is so large. I think few northerners are aware of how much more they are paying in food than do others in America. We tend to look on food inflation as a national menace and blame it on national and international market factors. It is quite true that the overall upward trend in food expenses is due to such forces, but the local disparity between North and South is due to a network of federal regulatory policies which force up prices in the Northeast and depress them in the rest of the country.

One night in 1976 I stayed overnight on a visit to Washington at the home of Aileen Gorman, president of the National Consumers' Congress, an organization that arose from the meat boycott of 1973 when consumers rebelled against staggering increases in the cost of beef by refusing to buy meat until the prices came down. Through her national network of contacts, Aileen was in a unique position to understand the nature of the problems facing the northeastern consumer at the supermarket. As we talked half the night, a portrait of unbelievable federally inspired price discrimination against the Northeast began to emerge. It became clear that the high prices I had encountered at the A&P in my neighborhood were caused by the deliberate bias of federal regulatory policies.

The most serious example of this bias is the regulatory policy of the Interstate Commerce Commission (ICC), created by the Interstate Commerce Act in 1887 to regulate the nation's rail and then truck commercial transportation network. Initially, the ICC was seen as a reform to bring laissez-faire capitalism in the commercial transportation area under public oversight and control. However, as is often the case with regulatory agencies, it was soon molded by industry to meet its needs. Today, few truckers and fewer unions would countenance an end to the ICC regulatory umbrella, shielding them from competition and true pressure to reduce rates and fees.

The essence of the ICC regulation of truckers is its power to approve the shipment of commodities by truck across state lines. Anyone wishing to transport clothing from New York to Boston, for example, must seek an ICC license to do so and must indicate over what route he proposes to make the shipment. Without an ICC license, it is unlawful to transport these commodities and the ICC uses its licensing power to control competition and assure, according to ICC defenders, adequate service to all parts of the country.

Under the terms of the ICC enabling legislation, unprocessed and unpackaged fruits, vegetables, and other foods are not subject to commission regulation and may be shipped without a license. This exception derives from the pressure of farmers to avoid the constraints and controls of federal regulation in getting their goods to markets throughout the country. This exception creates a class of "unregulated" truckers, that is, those who carry unpackaged foods and do not need ICC licenses alongside the "regulated" truckers who carry most other products.

The problem is that the ICC refuses to grant licenses to any "unregulated" trucker. Thus, if a trucker ships oranges from Florida to New York, he cannot get an ICC license to ship anything back from New York to Florida, and since there are no unpackaged fruit or other foods in New York for shipment to Florida, the trucker usually has to make the thousand-mile trip empty. The result is clear: The New

Yorkers buying Florida oranges have to pay not just for one-way transportation, but for two-way transportation, since the trucker could not get any cargo with which to offset the price of his return trip.

But it doesn't work the other way around. If a trucker wants to ship typewriters from New York to Florida, he can apply for and get an ICC license to do so. Having carried typewriters one way, he can either apply for a license to ship an ICC-regulated commodity back to New York or can take oranges back, an unregulated commodity. The Floridians do not have to pay for round-trip transportation when they buy typewriters, since the trucker can easily find a commodity to ship back to New York to pay for the return trip.[3]

By not permitting truckers who ship farm goods to cities the right to compete on equal terms for ICC licenses with truckers who carry other products, the ICC forces up food prices in American cities. Urban areas must pay twice for the transportation of all of their food, a stricture that does not apply to shippers of any other commodity to any other location.

The bias of the ICC regulation is clearly prorural. The rural area has plenty of raw foods to ship back to the urban area. It can always find a cargo for a truck so as to spare its residents the cost of having to pay for two-way transportation. But the urban community has no such luck. All of the commodities it might ship are regulated by the ICC. Thus, when a truck unloads food in an urban area, it is unlikely that it can find a cargo to ship back. Of course, if the ICC relaxed its regulations, it would become quite possible to offset the cost of the return trip and find a full cargo, but as long as the ICC arbitrarily bars truckers who ship food in one direction from shipping anything other than food in the return direction, the trucker must leave the city emptyhanded. Of course, the trucker pulling into a rural community with a full load has no such problem. He can readily find a food cargo to ship back and, failing that, can always obtain a license to ship a regulated cargo on his return trip.

Together, these restraints force a higher food bill in cities than in rural areas. The result of this bureaucratic nightmare is that food prices in New York, Boston, Philadelphia, and other northeastern cities are inflated by as much as 10 percent due to higher trucking costs. The effect of the ICC regulations is to drive up the cost to the urban consumer of buying food shipped from rural areas while leaving unaffected the cost to rural consumers of buying manufactured goods made in urban areas. A recent study by the Federal Highway Administration proves this point. The federal agency stopped a random sample of almost 70,000 trucks on large interstate highways and examined them to see if they were empty or carrying cargoes. Trucks classified as "unregulated"—carriers of unprocessed foods—were almost twice as likely to be empty as those classified as "regulated"—carriers of manufactured and other more urban products.

COMPARATIVE PERCENTAGE OF EMPTY TRUCKS ON INTERSTATE ROADS[4]

Truck Type	*Number Studied*	*% of Nonregulated Trucks Empty*	*% of Regulated Trucks Empty*
Van	40,585	32	19
Flat bed	18,437	38	29
Refrigerated van	11,730	38	20

Why does the ICC prohibit shipping an unregulated cargo one way and a regulated cargo the other way? The ICC says, simply enough, that they are not in the business of helping unregulated truckers take away business from regulated truckers. They are there to protect the business of the regulated truckers and keep cargoes for them. The ICC, as a matter of policy, tries to stop truckers who ship unregulated cargo one way from shipping regulated cargo the other way thereby "stealing" the business from a trucker who is willing to subject himself to ICC regulation in both trips. Nowhere is there a clearer example of the tangled world of Washington regulator and regulated working together to protect each other and keep the game going. It is absolutely incredible that at the height of the energy crisis, with transportation costs so high and gasoline so scarce, that a federal agency should be encouraging trucks to return empty from their destinations merely so as to preserve the ICC bureaucratic hegemony.[5]

Of course, the ICC's desire to protect its own regulatory turf is only one reason for the empty return trips. More important is the desire of truckers and the powerful Teamsters Union to preserve the extra work for trucking firms. If a situation is created in which urban food purchasers have to pay for empty return trips by the trucks that brought them their food, more work is created for the truckers who carry the cargoes the food trucks would have taken with them on their return trips, had the ICC permitted them to do so. The Teamsters Union is a powerful political force going back to the days of Dave Beck and Jimmy Hoffa. I recently worked with a New York congressman, normally a vigorous liberal, on the ICC's regulatory policies and urged him to speak up publicly about their impact on New York food prices. When I briefed him in his home on the issue, he was interested, engaged, and determined to press it publicly. He asked me to meet with a friend of his in the trucking business to check out my facts. The friend was an ICC-regulated trucker who confirmed my facts but opposed any change in the current regulatory scheme on the grounds that he couldn't weather the competition that would result if unregulated truckers could compete with regulated truckers for trucking business out of cities.

When I went back to my client—the New York congressman—he had completely changed his attitude. No longer was he interested in the issue. It was, he said, "not my field." He did not feel "adequately grounded in the area" to engage in a public debate over the issue of truck regulation. He paid me for my time, but chose not to use any of the material I had gathered. I took the facts to another New York congressman with whom I had worked closely over the years and who had willingly worked with me on a number of issues that other politicians found too dangerous to touch, but he too wasn't interested in taking on the truckers and the Teamsters. He let the memorandum I submitted to him lie on his desk for weeks and then told me when I asked that it wasn't up his alley.

If I was puzzled and incensed by the system the ICC uses to drive up trucking costs for food shipment to urban areas, I was absolutely amazed at the way milk prices are driven up by the equally incredible regulations of the Department of Agriculture. Here it is both the Northeast and the Sun Belt that suffer and the Midwest and Great Lakes states that benefit, but the impact of federal regulation is again clearly inflationary and wholly unwarranted. Once again, I went to a number of congressmen with the issue and all refused to touch it for fear of retribution by the powerful dairy interests in the Northeast.

Under current regulations, the Department of Agriculture sets minimum prices for milk in each area of the country. It bases these prices on the cost of what it calls "class 2 milk," that is, milk that is suitable for use in milk products but not for direct consumption. The department sets a price floor for the milk we drink for each area tied to the cost of refining milk from class 2 to class 1 and to the cost of transporting the milk from the dairy heartland of Wisconsin and Minnesota to the area in which the milk is sold.

Here's the catch: The adjustment for transportation is made even if the cost is not real. Thus, milk that is shipped from upstate New York to New York City—a distance of one hundred miles—is subject to the same price level as milk that is shipped a thousand miles. Thus, the Northeast's one major agricultural commodity—dairy products—must be sold to northeastern customers at the same markup for transportation costs as if they were imported into the region from Wisconsin and Minnesota. As fuel costs rise and labor costs escalate, the cost of this transportation becomes ever more important as an element in dairy prices. Its significance is indicated by a comparison of milk prices in the Northeast and the Midwest:

MILK PRICES FOR CLASS 1 MILK IN SELECTED CITIES[6]

Northeast		*Midwest*	
Boston	$11.22	Milwaukee	$9.64
Philadelphia	11.28	Chicago	9.70
Hartford	11.42	Indianapolis	9.91
Baltimore	11.22	Des Moines	9.84

Aileen Gorman underscores the discriminatory effect of this system of federal marketing orders for milk: "The net effect of this nexus of government regulation is to increase sharply the price for the consumer. Consumers end up paying for transportation that may not actually happen and for government regulations that need not exist except as a sop to the transportation industry."

The dramatic effect of government regulation in driving up food industry prices has often been discussed by those who favor a loosening of the government's regulatory reins. But the geographic nature of this discrimination has not received due attention. The Northeast must import all its food—mostly by truck—from other regions of the country. Any regulation or system that acts to increase the cost of that transportation has a uniquely discriminatory and inflationary effect on the Northeast. There is really only one basic food commodity that the Northeast produces in relative abundance: dairy products. But the federal regulatory framework assures that we pay for the transportation of the one commodity we need not import in such quantity by building the cost of the transportation into the cost of the product and requiring that it stay there through federal regulation.

When we go to the supermarket in our northeastern urban locales, we must take care to differentiate that price inflation which is due to market and worldwide supply-and-demand forces and that which is due directly to federal policies that force up the prices we must pay in the urban Northeast for our food. The entire nation faces the problem of rapidly inflating food prices, but the Northeast faces it worse than any other part of America due to the actions of the Interstate Commerce Commission and the Department of

Agriculture in protecting a system of transportation featherbedding in the trucking and milk industries.

Together with the discriminatory handling of the energy crisis, the inflation of food costs at the behest of federal policy has forced living costs in the Northeast to rise beyond all proportion to those in the rest of the nation. As will be discussed later in this book, these higher costs of living in the Northeast directly lead to an erosion of our economic well-being. They assure that we pay more in taxes, get less in aid and services from the federal government, lose industry faster, have a slower rate of economic growth, and are less attractive economically than the rest of the nation. Many assume that the higher cost of living in the Northeast is due to market forces and historical trends beyond the control of local and even of national government. This is just not true. The two key elements of this higher local cost of living—energy and food—are directly due to federal policies. The third major cause of this cost disparity is the expense of state and local government, and, as we have seen, these costs are inflating due to forces quite beyond the control of local governments and certainly beyond the control of the liberals who run them.

In all, the economic decay and deterioration of the Northeast are largely attributable to factors far beyond its immediate sphere of control or even of influence. The following chapters will discuss how federal *budgetary* policies add to the impact of the discrimination we have already discussed in federal *regulatory* policies to further the discomfort and economic malaise of the northeastern American city.

7.

HOW THE NORTHEAST LOSES ITS MONEY

The juxtaposition was quite dramatic. I sat in the gallery of the New York City Council in June 1975 to watch it adopt a budget destined to bring pain and suffering on New York's citizens through layoffs, wage freezes, and other austerity measures to cut city spending and avoid default. As the debate droned on like a collective, muted, hopeless wail of agony at the cuts and reductions in vital services the budget foreshadowed, I pondered a blue book in my lap entitled *Summary of Federal Outlays in New York State: 1974*. The report had just been issued by the United States Department of Commerce and contained a geographic breakout of all federal spending, pinpointing how much federal money from which programs went to which counties in the state of New York and, in other volumes, to each of the other forty-nine states.[1]

I felt enraged as I added up the numbers. Here, the New York City Council was prepared to enact a budget that would lead to a reduction of almost 20 percent in the city's municipal labor force including a 10 percent cut in the Police and Fire Departments and a cut of almost 25 percent in the teacher force. While these cuts were under discussion, each City Council member must have been conscious of the fact that New York City is the most highly taxed locality in the nation, with a stiff income tax, an 8 percent sales tax, a high property tax, and an array of business and consumer taxes without equal in the nation. New York City was being castigated for "living beyond its means," and its local political leaders were finally recognizing, under the duress of federal pressure, the need to cut that edifice of social and human concerns erected over the past forty years. The concepts of aid to the poor and service to citizens developed over the years by Alfred E. Smith, Franklin D. Roosevelt, Fiorello La Guardia, Herbert Lehman, Robert Wagner, and John Lindsay were to be erased in an orgy of budget cuts puncuated by the slogan that New York must "balance" its budget.

But in my lap lay a report that showed that New York State pays to the federal government $36 billion in tax revenues every year but gets back from Washington only $24 billion in government spending of all sorts. The data indicated that the city of New York sent to Washington almost $10 billion more than it received in federal spending.[2] This locality, struggling for its very fiscal life, was sending the federal government a vastly greater sum in taxes than it was receiving from Washington in spending; it was subsidizing the rest of America.

Nor was New York unique in this subsidization of the federal government. Later that day, I went to La Guardia Airport to fly to Ohio to meet with Richard Celeste, that state's liberal Democratic lieutenant governor, to discuss some issue papers I had prepared for him on Ohio's Medicaid program. En route, I examined the data for Ohio and found that it had contributed $17 billion in federal taxes but received only $11 billion in federal spending. I shared the data with Celeste, who was visibly shocked by it. It seemed that nobody quite understood the magnitude of what was happening to the Northeast at the hands of the federal budget and why.

Ever since the Kennedy administration, we have changed our national notion of the impact of federal spending on our economy. We have become a nation of Keynesians accepting the doctrine enunciated by the economist John Maynard Keynes that government spending should exceed government taxation in times of recession to "prime the pump" and stimulate consumer buying power. Conversely, we accept the notion that when government taxes exceed government spending, there is a net outflow of money from the economy which tends to cool off the economy and slow the pace of economic expansion. Viewed in this light, the data concerning federal spending and taxation patterns in New York, Ohio, and the rest of the Northeast assume a quite different dimension. Not only is it unfair for the federal government to tax the Northeast so much more heavily than is its level of spending there, but it is extremely deleterious to the region's economy.

So massive is the shortchange in federal spending, so pervasive the imbalance between federal spending in the Northeast and federal tax collections from it, that one must go well beyond considerations of justice or fairness. Indeed, the federal government is guilty of pursuing two diametrically opposite fiscal policies. Toward the Northeast it offers a rigid, restrictive policy, taxing far more than it offers in spending, taking wealth out of the region's economy depleting consumer buying power. Toward the Sun Belt, it offers a policy of massive pump-priming and deficit spending, taking far less in taxes than it puts back in spending. To one part of this nation, Washington preaches the economics of expansion, of growth, while to the Northeast it offers those of restriction, recession, and sluggishness. My own calculations, since reprinted in the excellent work by Jack Newfield and Paul DeBrul *The Abuse of Power,*[3] were close to those developed by the *National Journal*[4] in a similar research effort. The magnitude of the imbalance between federal spending and taxation in the Northeast and in the Sun Belt still startles me every time I have occasion to reread the data.[5]

FEDERAL TAXES AND FEDERAL SPENDING IN THE NORTHEAST AND SUNBELT COMPARED, 1975

Northeast

State	*Federal Taxes (in millions)*	*Federal Spending (in millions)*	*Surplus (+)/ Deficit (–) (in millions)*
Maine	$ 760	$ 1,277	+ 517
Massachusetts	7,622	8,474	+ 852
Vermont	319	641	+ 322
Connecticut	5,946	5,137	– 809
New Hampshire	714	1,145	+ 431
Rhode Island	1,204	1,243	+ 39
New York	39,007	24,269	–14,738
New Jersey	11,083	8,395	– 2,688
Pennsylvania	17,697	14,462	– 3,235
Ohio	17,194	10,822	– 6,372
Indiana	6,860	5,412	– 1,448
Illinois	21,774	13,462	– 8,312
Michigan	14,778	9,095	– 5,683
Minnesota	6,150	4,497	– 1,653
Wisconsin	5,422	4,443	– 979
TOTAL	$156,530	$112,774	–43,756

Sun Belt

State	*Federal Taxes (in millions)*	*Federal Spending (in millions)*	*Surplus (+)/ Deficit (–) (in millions)*
Virginia	$ 5,035	$ 8,906	+ 3,871
North Carolina	1,875	6,100	+ 4,225
Tennessee	3,511	5,425	+ 1,914
South Carolina	1,875	3,485	+ 1,610
Georgia	4,784	6,786	+ 2,002
Florida	7,787	11,512	+ 3,725
Alabama	2,684	4,816	+ 2,132
Mississippi	1,167	3,740	+ 2,573
Louisiana	3,287	4,596	+ 1,309
Texas	16,048	15,806	– 242
Arkansas	1,241	2,544	+ 1,303
Oklahoma	3,361	3,871	+ 510
Arizona	1,789	3,646	+ 1,857
New Mexico	708	2,264	+ 1,556
California	28,510	35,838	+ 7,328
TOTAL	$83,662	$119,335	+35,673

When one examines these numbers, it is small wonder that the Northeast region in general and New York in particular are in serious economic trouble. If Keynes was at all right in his assertion that an excess of government taxes over government spending tends to retard economic growth, then the economic problems of the Northeast are truly explainable by federal fiscal policies. The Sun Belt is booming, not because of its supposedly vaunted qualities of enterprise and capitalist initiative, but because it gets $36 billion more in federal spending than it has to pay in taxes. Similarly, the Northeast is slumping not because of its climate, labor unions, crime, pollution, minority groups, or its liberalism, but because it is paying $44 billion more in federal taxes than it gets in federal spending.

In other words, about one dollar in fifteen in the Northeast's regional economy is sent to Washington in taxes and never returns.[6] The New York City Council may have to wrestle with a "deficit" in the local New York City budget—that is, an excess of spending over revenues. But New York City is not in a deficit at all when one considers not only local but national and state spending and revenues as well. The fact is that New Yorkers pay the federal, state, and local governments vastly more in taxes than they receive from these three levels of government, combined, in spending. New York's local deficit is offset by huge surpluses (outflows) at the federal level.

Manhattan Borough President Percy Sutton asked me to quantify the total amount that all New Yorkers pay in taxes to all levels of government and to compare it with the total amount that they receive in spending from all levels of government. He asked that I undertake the same calculation for Atlanta, Dallas, and Houston to compare their fiscal situation with New York's. My conclusion was important and startling: that New York was the only one of the four cities that was taxed more than it received in spending. All the others lived off a net *inflow* of money: New York had a net *outflow*.

COMPARISON OF GOVERNMENT TAXES AND SPENDING IN FOUR CITIES[7]

City	*Level of Government*	*Taxes*	*Spending*	*Outflow (–) Inflow (+)*
New York	Federal	$ 19.8 billion	$ 10.8 billion	$+ 9.0 billion
	State	3.6 billion	3.2 billion	+ .4 billion
	City	5.5 billion	9.1 billion	– 3.6 billion
	TOTAL	$ 28.9 billion	$ 23.1 billion	$+ 5.8 billion
Houston	Federal	$1,563 million	$1,475 million	$+ 88 million
	State	247 million	398 million	– 151 million
	County	58 million	59 million	– 1 million
	City	204 million	182 million	+ 22 million
	TOTAL	$2,072 million	$2,114 million	$– 42 million
Dallas	Federal	$1,075 million	$1,412 million	$– 337 million
	State	224 million	246 million	– 22 million
	County	32 million	98 million	– 66 million
	City	180 million	185 million	– 5 million
	TOTAL	$1,511 million	$1,941 million	$– 430 million
Atlanta	Federal	$ 483 million	$1,412 million	$– 929 million
	State	103 million	199 million	– 96 million
	County	62 million	70 million	– 8 million
	City	141 million	143 million	– 2 million
	TOTAL	$ 789 million	$1,824 million	$–1,035 million

Thus, the budgets of Houston, Dallas, and Atlanta appear to be in almost perfect balance, each city taking in enough revenues to offset fully its level of spending. By contrast, the New York City budget appears to be dramatically out of balance with revenues running substantially behind expenses. But when taxes to *all* governments—state, federal, county, and local—are measured against spending by *all* governments, the three southern cities spend substantially more than they take in in taxes while New York must pay more in taxes than it receives in spending.

In general, the staggering outflow of our wealth through federal budgetary policy makes real economic progress in the Northeast quite impossible. We swim against a mighty current generated by federal fiscal policies which work to push us backward. More particularly, the disparity between the way the federal spending pattern treats the Northeast as opposed to the Sun Belt raises an even broader conceptual question: Are the Congress and the administration thinking too much of *national* as opposed to *regional* economic policies? Are we not too often distracted by discussion of the size of the federal deficit or surplus and of its economic impact from a consideration of the extent to which that deficit or surplus distributes itself evenly throughout the nation? Why, indeed, are the figures in this book or those completed by a slightly different methodology in the *National Journal* worthy of publication? The mere fact that to my knowledge no source at any level of government routinely makes and publishes such regional comparison underscores the lack of attention to the widely varying impact of federal spending and tax policies.

I was surprised by the interest with which my findings and those of the *National Journal* were greeted by congressmen and senators from the Northeast. All were vaguely aware of a shortchange in dealings with Washington, but none were aware of its extent or the disparity between the southern and northern experience. One concludes that we just don't look at our economy as a series of regions, each subject to different economic conditions and the object of different degrees of federal stimulation. This blind spot in our economic analyses leads us to make terrible mistakes without even realizing that we have made them.

The Congress, for example, does not chart out in each year's budget how much will be the deficit or the surplus in each area of the nation. The Congressional Budget Committee and the Office of Management and Budget dicker about the size of the national deficit or surplus, but little or no attention is given to its geographic allocation. Except for sporadic scrutiny, the spending decisions of individual federal agencies are not reviewed as to their geographic distribution and consequent economic effect. Of course, federal spending is often governed by formulae which prescribe the geographic distribution of the aid. But less than one quarter of the federal budget is governed by such formulae.[8] The rest is determined by bureaucratic, individual, or business decisions having nothing to do with any geographic prescription for federal outlays.

Perhaps it is a fear of balkanization which inhibits regional economic planning—fear of dividing the nation against itself. Yet, a regional approach to fiscal policy planning is quite the opposite. It is an effort to understand more profoundly the correct economic policy by informing a national point of view with more knowledge of how each of America's regional components must be treated to accommodate balanced and coordinated national growth. Ironically, the absence of any overall framework for making national decisions about the geographic distribution of federal spending encourages a political tug of war between regions, a contest whose outcome is likely to be determined more by congressional seniority or presidential politics than by economic merit.

In the aftermath of the Nixon-Ford-Agnew years, one can wonder to what extent this pattern of federal discrimination in spending and taxes is an economic concomitant of the vaunted "southern strategy"—the Nixon effort to play to the politics of the supposedly permanent Republican Sun Belt and western majority as opposed to the urban Northeast and Great Lakes states. We haven't found a "smoking gun" yet—no direct evidence of any plot to rob one region to benefit another. Obviously, many of the policies that caused this imbalance pre-date 1968. There is no evidence that tax laws were altered to cause a disparity in federal budget impact on the Northeast and on the Sun Belt. But there is some basis for believing that certain aspects of federal budgetary bias have their roots in deliberate policy choices in the Nixon White House. It is hard to conjecture, for example, that the states of the Sun Belt, with 38 percent of the national population, ended up with 50 percent of the defense budget and 53 percent of the nation's military installations by happenstance. (See Chapter 9 for details.) Similarly, the antiurban housing record of the Republican years is hard to dismiss as coincidence.

This book is not designed to prove a conspiratorial view of how a regional imbalance happened; it is merely to document what has occurred and to trace some of the causes and possible areas in which we might look for solutions. It is my hope that before we discuss "business climate" or weaken that nexus of laws and customs that have made the northern city the hope of millions of migrants and immigrants over the years, we probe more deeply this financial assault, from Washington, on our region's economy and its prospects for survival. A large part of this book is devoted to a sketch of the basic elements of this federal budgetary discrimination. The process by which Washington takes from the Northeast $44 billion more in taxes than it generates in spending is a complex one. Its ingredients include federal tax law, cash transfer payments, federal air formulae, and defense spending. Although we cannot explore each aspect of the federal laws, we can hopefully suggest the basic directions in which to look.

8.

THE DISCRIMINATORY FEDERAL INCOME TAX

All Americans are subject to the same federal tax laws regardless of where they live, so it might at first appear incongruous to speak of the discriminatory impact of federal income taxation. Yet just as we have come to understand that federal tax laws discriminate in favor of the wealthy and against the wage earner, it is also true that the complex network of deductions, credits, and preferences accorded by the tax laws work to the advantage of the Sun Belt taxpayer and against the urban northeasterner. Indeed, so discriminatory are these tax laws that the citizens of New York City pay 6.8 percent of the nation's personal income tax collections, although they constitute only 3.6% of the nation's population.[1]

Consider the difference between the daily lives of the southern rural resident and his northern urban counterpart. The rural southerner likely owns his own home and the urban northeasterner probably rents his dwelling. As a homeowner, the southerner can deduct the money he pays the bank for interest on his mortgage and the funds he pays his local government in property taxes. The northerner, as a tenant, cannot avail himself of either of these deductions since he does not own the dwelling in which he lives. The southerner probably drives to work while the northerner is more likely to use mass transit. In using his automobile, the southerner can deduct his gasoline taxes, but the northerner cannot deduct any part of his transportation cost.

The southerner lives in a low cost-of-living area. According to the Bureau of Labor Statistics, it costs only $19,442 to live in a southern rural community at the same standard as costs $29,677 in New York City.[2] If we assume that each has the same standard of living, and therefore one makes $19,442 and the other $29,677 a year, it is clear that the New Yorker will pay more in income taxes because he has a higher income, despite the fact that this higher income exists only on paper; it is more than offset, in reality, by the higher living costs the New Yorker must pay. In fact, the $29,677 New York income will put the city family in a 27 percent tax bracket while the $19,442 southern income will put it in a 22 percent tax bracket. Each, in effect, earns the same amount, can buy the same amount, and lives at the same standard, but one is in a higher tax bracket than the other.

In all, the southerner lives under a tax law designed to help him pay less in taxes while the urban northerner lives under a tax law that tries to maximize his payments. The higher tax levels in northern as opposed to southern communities has long been a national fact of life. According to the federal government, for example, the high-income New York family pays $7,976 in taxes while the high-income Dallas, Texas, family pays only $2,980.[3] But we tend to blame the higher taxes in the North on state and local governments. Liberal overspending, welfare policies, high health care costs, and other government budgetary burdens are cited as the reason for the high taxes the urban northerner must pay. But the fact is that state and local taxes in the Northeast are *not* the key reason for the higher tax burdens in the North; *federal* taxes are the reason. The fact that a New Yorker might pay more in taxes than a Texan is due primarily to the discrimination inherent in the operations of the federal income tax, and only in part to the higher level of local government spending in New York as opposed to Texas.

Indeed, taxes, as a percentage of personal income, do not fluctuate very dramatically over different regions of the nation:

STATE AND LOCAL TAXES AS A PERCENT OF PERSONAL INCOME[4]

Northeast		Sun Belt	
Region	*% of Income*	*Region*	*% of Income*
New England	15.8	Southeast	15.3
Mideast	17.3	Southwest	14.3
Great Lakes	14.6		
National Average: 15.6%			

By contrast, *federal* per capita tax burdens vary more from state to state. The average northerner pays $1,727 in federal taxes, 27.8 percent of his income, while the average southerner pays only $1,415, 25.5 percent of his income. Look at how much higher the average federal tax payment is in northern as opposed to southern states:

PER CAPITA FEDERAL TAX BURDEN, 1977[5]

Northeast		Sun Belt	
State	*Per Capita Federal Tax Burden*	*State*	*Per Capita Federal Tax Burden*
Connecticut	$2,073	California	$1,711
New Jersey	1,957	Virginia	1,499
Illinois	1,907	Florida	1,490
New York	1,850	Texas	1,393
Massachusetts	1,711	Arizona	1,332
Michigan	1,701	Georgia	1,321

Northeast		Sun Belt	
State	*Per Capita Federal Tax Burden*	*State*	*Per Capita Federal Tax Burden*
Rhode Island	1,669	Oklahoma	1,262
Ohio	1,629	Tennessee	1,291
Pennsylvania	1,602	North Carolina	1,260
Indiana	1,497	Louisiana	1,200
Wisconsin	1,488	South Carolina	1,179
Minnesota	1,479	Alabama	1,145
New Hampshire	1,478	New Mexico	1,103
Vermont	1,338	Arkansas	1,069
Maine	1,252	Mississippi	964
NORTHEAST AVERAGE	$1,727	SUN BELT AVERAGE	$1,415
U.S. Average: 1,565			

When the federal income tax was first imposed in its current form in 1917, the concept of a graduated income tax took hold as the basis for federal revenue raising. The idea behind the tax was simple: that those with higher incomes should pay a higher tax and a higher percentage of their incomes in taxes. As originally imposed, the income tax was the culmination of decades of progressive efforts to tax to sustain government based on wealth rather than on consumption, property, or other criteria. Under a pure graduated income tax system, or course, taxes would increase as the ability to pay them rose, setting up an equitable and liberal method of financing government.

In the intervening years, two trends were set in motion to pollute this pure income tax notion and create the relatively unfair and somewhat illiberal system with which we struggle today:

- A host of special deductions, shelters, and exemptions were granted certain taxpayers in an effort to encourage homeowning, certain types of investment, and vindicate other social and economic purposes.
- Inflation set in, driving up costs throughout the nation, but increasing them more substantially in northern than in southern areas of the nation. Thus, the income tax, which taxed dollar income, was no longer taxing based on the ability to pay (that is, the standard of living) but on nominal dollar income—an

income whose actual purchasing power fluctuated wildly from area to area.

The network of exemptions, deductions, and shelters that has grown in the years since 1917 has come under increasing fire recently as prejudicial to the needs of the middle class and the poor and unduly protective of the wealthy, whose large amounts of capital enable them to invest their funds so as to capitalize on the tax privileges written into the law. But little attention has been paid to the geographic distribution of these special benefits. The fact is that not only do these tax provisions reward the rich but they also reward the rural and the southern American at the expense of his urban and northern counterpart.

Similarly, the inability of the tax system to take account of differences in the value of the dollar from North to South and from rural to urban areas dictates an unduly large level of tax payment in the North, a payment level reflective not of actual wealth or buying power but of the higher cost of living to which the northerner is subject. The net effect of these two discriminatory features of the income tax system is that the northerner pays more in taxes than his just share. Although the *real* per capita income, adjusted for cost-of-living differences, in the North is only 2 percent higher than in the South, the average northerner pays 22 percent more in federal income taxes. For example, New York State's real per capita income is actually 3 percent *less* that of Georgia, but New Yorkers pay over $500 more per capita in federal income taxes than do Georgians.[6]

It is important to explore how the higher northern cost of living combines with the discriminatory nature of the special deductions and shelters in the tax code to elicit greater tax payments from the Northeast and permit lesser payments by the Sun Belt.

THE INCOME TAX AND THE COST OF LIVING

In early 1976 I briefed Manhattan Borough President Percy Sutton on my data concerning the discriminatory features of the income tax as it affected the Northeast. "I think we ought to sue to challenge the constitutionality of the income tax system," Sutton replied. What an idea! Sutton's contention was simple. The income tax taxed a New Yorker making $29,500 and a Texan making $21,500 in different tax brackets. The New Yorker appears to be richer, but a close review of his expenses and those incurred in Dallas indicates that each can live at exactly the same standard of living, even though the New Yorker earns $8,000 more each year. Sutton argued that it violated the Fourteenth Amendment to tax two people making the same *real* income at different rates just because their *nominal* income appeared to be greater. It was a fascinating contention. As his mind, trained as a civil rights lawyer, pondered the legal action, I wondered how we could make the court understand that the income tax system had become unconstitutional. Oddly enough, it used to be perfectly legal and equitable. But the energy crisis, federal food price regulations, and a host of recent developments have opened up huge cost-of-living differences in this country which have rendered unconstitutional a tax system that takes no account of these differences.

We are used to thinking of inflation as a national trend. We listen to the quarterly reports of the Bureau of Labor Statistics and the Department of Commerce itemizing changes in the Consumer Price Index. We have come to accept these quotations as having some meaning; we think of them as we think of the Dow-Jones stock market averages or the unemployment rate. But implicit in such measurements is the unstated assumption that we are one nation, experiencing inflation uniformly, rising and falling together, grumbling together about prices, and reaching together ever deeper into our pocketbooks. Unfortunately, another publication of the Bureau of Labor Statistics receives less publicity. Every quarter the bureau publishes its estimate of what it costs to sustain a high-, moderate-, and low-income standard of living in different regions of America.

The bureau assumes that a family of four rents or owns a certain amount of living space in each region, eats an identical diet, has a certain need for medical care, pays certain taxes, and incurs expenses connected with an identical standard of living. Its researchers add up the costs associated with maintaining such a standard of living in the different metropolitan areas of the nation and concludes what is a reasonable "budget" to sustain such a level of existence in each area. Were the results of the bureau's calculations more widely read, it would open a whole new spectrum in which to examine the problems of the urban Northeast. We would begin to understand that living costs vary dramatically throughout the nation and that the effect of inflation is, in reality, most unequal.

According to the Bureau of Labor Statistics, it costs $19,384 to live in Boston at exactly the same level, exactly the same standard of living that costs only $13,855 in a southern rural area. Compare the differences in living costs in the Northeast as opposed to the Sun Belt for a family of four living at an intermediate standard of living as defined by the bureau:

INTERMEDIATE INCOME LIVING COSTS[7]

Northeast		*Sun Belt*	
Region	*Cost*	*Region*	*Cost*
Boston	$19,384	Houston	$14,978
New York	18,866	Atlanta	14,830
Milwaukee	17,307	Dallas	14,699
Philadelphia	16,836	Southwest rural	14,627
Chicago	16,651	Southern rural	13,855

That we actually can consider ourselves to live under one currency system after noting such mammoth differences is a remarkable feat of mental jugglery. The differences in the purchasing power of the southern and the northern dollar are so significant, so substantial, that they approximate the differences between the values of two foreign currencies. Indeed, the gap between the buying power of a dollar, at a high level of income, in a southern rural area and in Boston actually approach the difference between the purchasing power of a French franc and a German Deutschmark.

The northern dollar is worth far less than the southern dollar. Almost every American tourist has probably had the experience of paying for goods in the wrong currency as he shuttles from country to country in a two- or three-week tour of Europe. If one happens to be paying in a cheaper currency, the proprietors are likely to smile and accept the more valuable currency cheerfully without pointing out the mistake. I have had the experience of getting a scornful look from a Parisian shopkeeper whom I was about to pay, mistakenly, in less valuable Belgian—instead of French—francs. From then on, I traveled with my currencies clearly divided in my wallet and a converter ever ready for a quick calculation.

But we mix northern and southern dollars freely. In some areas, the northern dollar has purchasing power a full forty cents less than does the southern dollar, but our tax laws take no account of the difference. In fact, not only do they take no account of this difference, but the tax laws act to rub salt in our wounds. When liberals over the years fashioned the income tax structure we have today, their idea was very simple and very sound: Let income tax rates vary so that the higher one's income, the more one pays in taxes. Indeed, the higher one's income, the higher *percentage* of it one paid in taxes. It was a radical notion then and, if ever really applied, without loopholes, is an important idea today. But the income tax was fashioned in an atmosphere of relatively equal living costs in different parts of America. Of course, there were minor differences, but the rapid, rampant inflation of the late sixties and early seventies had yet to transform the value of the dollar and the energy crisis had yet to reap its highly geographically selective harm. When rapid inflation was upon us—more rapid in the North than in the South—living-cost differences began to emerge. The liberal theory behind the income tax was obvious in its intent—tax the rich more heavily. But its wording referred not to wealth or ability to purchase goods and services, but only to actual dollar income. This wording meant that one did not just tax the rich more heavily, but that one taxed more heavily as well those who appeared to be richer because of their residence in high cost-of-living areas.

How ironic that a liberal notion—progressively graduated income taxes—should be turned against the liberal Northeast. Herbert Hoover predicted that if Franklin Roosevelt was ever elected, he would so raise the income tax that "grass would grow in the streets of a thousand cities." He was quite right, but for reasons quite at variance with the liberal notions of the Roosevelt administration.

Unfortunately for the northeastern economy, the higher one's income goes, the more dramatic the differences between the tax one pays in the North and in the South. This is for two reasons: First, the income tax is steeply graduated. The higher an income, the more rapid the rate of increase in the percentage of it one must pay in taxes. Secondly, differences between southern and northern costs of living are more and more accentuated the higher the income levels compared. So a New Yorker earning $50,000 likely has the same buying power as a Texan earning only $36,000. Under the tax law, the New Yorker will end up paying 37 percent of his income in taxes while the Texan need only part with 31 percent of his income each year. In other words, the New Yorker must pay $3,000 more for the privilege of living in New York.

I agree heartily with the notion that ability to pay should be the major criteria in taxation. But let's not quibble about technicalities. The fact that a person makes more money than another person doesn't make him richer if his cost of living is higher. If his food, clothing, shelter, transportation, and other costs are 10 percent higher and his income is 10 percent higher, he is not richer than the other man—he is just as rich. There is no reason why he should be required to pay more in taxes.

Some sort of indexing of the income tax to account for regional gaps in living costs as reflected in Bureau of Labor Statistics data would appear to be an appropriate legislative remedy for the disparity in income tax burdens. The bureau's survey methods, which have been criticized in some quarters, could be reviewed to assure the fairness of its resulting indices. Then if a workable set of living-cost ratios were devised for different levels of income and different regions of the nation, these indices could be assimilated into the income tax form. Thus an upper-income family in New York would pay according to one schedule of rates while an upper-income family in Dallas would pay according to another schedule. The different schedules would be so adjusted as to eliminate the difference in tax rates for persons or families in different parts of the nation earning the same *real* income, but a nominally different income. We already have separate rates depending upon whether one is married or single or the head of a household. Different schedules could be printed depending upon one's place of residence.

Obviously, the political fallout from such a proposal would be severe. The system of regional compensations would lessen materially the tax burdens in the northeastern cities and their suburbs while raising the burden for southern and southwestern taxpayers. No doubt it would be met with strong Sun Belt resistance. But by raising the issue and pressing their case, the northeastern congressmen could secure modifications in the income tax formulae which would lessen the extent of their constituents' overpayment. At least, such adjustments would put billions of dollars back into the northeastern economy by reducing their level of taxation to one that more nearly approximated the rest of America. If the northeastern states paid federal taxes so adjusted for regional differences in their living costs, their total federal tax payments would decline by about $20-30 billion. So drastic an infusion of wealth into the northeastern economy could not help but revivify the entire region economically.[8]

Except for Sutton, few politicians have been willing to embrace the notion of indexing. I recently spoke, however, with the president of one of America's largest insurance companies—one located in New York. I outlined the problem of income tax discrimination to him and, before I could continue, he said, "I think the only real answer is some sort of indexing." I was startled. I had spoken to dozens of congressmen and several senators and none had advanced the notion of indexing and most were slow to grasp its importance. One congressman sent letters to four economists asking what they thought of the idea. The liberal economists, such as Robert Lekachman, replied with general support. Milton Friedman, the conservative economist from Chicago, denounced the idea. Indexing is a notion that is often foreign to American politicians, but it may be the only way to prevent the wholesale export of the Northeast's wealth amid regional cost-of-living differences and variations.

DISCRIMINATORY DEDUCTIONS

Charles Rangel is a Harlem congressman who sits on the all-powerful Ways and Means Committee in the House of Representatives. Rangel is an intelligent and dedicated black political leader who impressed the entire country for his sound and probing manner during the Nixon impeachment hearings as he sat on the House Judiciary Committee. Rangel takes tax reform seriously. He has mastered many of the complexities of the tax code and is a leader of the group of liberals who battle on the Ways and Means Committee—which controls tax legislation—for real reform. But he has never raised the issue of *geographic* discrimination. Like other liberals, he has been educated to watch for *economic* discrimination in the income tax, but not to notice how deductions and other facets of the tax law take money away from his Harlem constituents and move it to the Sun Belt and the South. The entire focus of tax reform has been on eliminating economic inequities that benefit the rich at the expense of the poor and the middle class, not on the geographic discrimination implicit in these same deductions and shelters, although the discrimination against the Northeast is at least as serious as that against the poor and middle class.

To begin with, the tax law grants a host of special deductions and exemptions for certain industries deemed to be in the national interest and in need of special tax advantages. Agriculture, for example, is permitted to avoid payment of $1.1 billion in income taxes through special tax benefits not accorded other industries.[9] Farmers are permitted to deduct certain costs as current expenses, even though these expenditures were for next year's crops or for capital improvements. In other businesses, such expenses could not be deducted, but in agriculture they can. Farmers can also treat income derived from the sale of livestock, orchards, vineyards, and other agricultural activities as a capital gain, not as ordinary income. Capital gains, normally reserved for profits on investments, are taxed at a lower rate than ordinary income. Thus, income for certain farmers can be taxed according to the lesser capital gains tax rate rather than the income tax rate other taxpayers must pay.

In 1976 oil, timber, coal, and other mining industries realized $2.9 billion in tax benefits permitting them to deduct capital costs as current operating expenses (instead of having to spread the costs over several years) and to realize depletion allowances to shelter their income from taxation.[10] These benefits are not accorded other industries and are crucial to the profitability of mining and lumbering as well as the oil industry. While depletion allowances are being phased out by congressional tax reform, billions of dollars of tax benefits remain in the law to assist these industries.

Agriculture and mining are, of course, rural industries, concentrated in the Sun Belt and the West and of only minimal importance in the Northeast. Yet these industries are singled out for special tax advantage, decreasing the total tax burden in rural areas and, to compensate for the lost revenue, increasing the tax burden in urban communities. By especially favoring these rural industries and not according similar advantage to those more likely to be situated in urban areas, the tax law gives an advantage to the rest of the nation which it denies to the urban Northeast.

The tax law aids homeowners but not tenants, another key antiurban bias. Those who own their own homes are permitted to deduct their property tax payments and their mortgage interest payments, deductions that permitted homeowners, in 1976, to avoid payment of $8.5 billion in federal income taxes.[11] But the Internal Revenue Service does not permit a tenant to deduct either his property taxes or the interest paid on the mortgage for the rental building in which he lives. This restriction stems from the theory that both property tax and mortgage interest are paid by the landlord or property owner. In fact, both are paid by the tenant in his rent, which the owner then uses to pay the bank and the government. But since the landlord actually writes the check, the tenant can take no deduction. The landlord, of course, can take a deduction, but it has no practical significance for the landlord, since he must report the rent paid him by the tenant as income in the first place. So if a landlord pays $10,000 in property taxes on his apartment building and receives the $10,000 from his tenants in rent, he must report to the IRS the receipt of $10,000 in income and the deduction of $10,000 in property tax payments. He derives no advantage from the deduction, since it is fully offset by the income he must report. If, on the other hand, the tenant were granted the deduction, he could realize the same advantage as is accorded homeowners: the deduction of property tax and mortgage interest payments from one's normal income for tax purposes. Since most rental housing is concentrated in cities, the arbitrary exclusion of tenant-paid property taxes and mortgage interest from the list of permissible deductions is a direct form of bias against cities. A tenant in an apartment building and a rural or suburban homeowner who pay identical property tax are treated differently. One receives a subsidy from Washington in the tax deduction he may take while the other is denied this aid.

The impact of this bias is tremendously significant. In New York City, for example, one dollar in forty of total personal income is paid by tenants in property taxes to the city government. Were these New York tenants permitted to deduct property taxes and mortgage interest payments on their income tax, about $2 billion of new deductions would be permitted. For the average tenant, the deduction of property taxes and mortgage interest would permit him to write off about 10 percent of his income as a tax deduction.[12]

The federal tax law permits gasoline taxes to be deducted on the federal income tax form. It does not permit taxes on utility bills or home heating oil or any other form of energy consumption to be deducted—only taxes on gasoline. Of course, gasoline consumption is much higher in rural than in urban areas. New York City, for example, has over 40 percent of New York State's people but only 20 percent of its cars.[13] By permitting a deduction for gasoline taxes and not for other energy taxes, the tax code rewards the rural energy user but not the urban one. President Carter is seeking to repeal this gasoline tax exemption and, hopefully, will be successful.

But it is even more subtle forms of bias against cities that make the tax code a particularly antiurban document. For example, once the Budd Corporation factory in Philadelphia was a center for the manufacture of auto replacement parts and truck bodies. Its thousands of jobs were vital to the Philadelphia economy and to the thousands of people they supported. When Budd decided to relocate their plant to Indiana and Canada, officials of the regional United Auto Workers were aghast. Budd had always been a mainstay of the Northeast's part of the auto industry and there seemed to be no reason for Budd to move out. Their plant needed some renovation and modernization, but both were possible without great dislocation and could be done for a small fraction of the cost of a new plant.

When Auto Workers officers met with representatives of the Budd Corporation, it became clear that, in the words of Ed Grey, regional director for the United Auto Workers, "federal tax breaks were a key part of Budd's decision to relocate much of its operation. The economics of leaving Philadelphia didn't make much sense unless you considered the edge that the company would get under the investment tax credit for relocating its facilities and putting up a new plant." A federal tax break—paid for by the citizens of

Philadelphia as much as any—was the key reason for the loss of vitally needed urban jobs.

The investment tax credit is a tax law provision allowing businesses to credit certain percentages of their total new investment in equipment and machinery against their tax bill. The investment credit, which cost the federal government $1.4 billion in taxes in 1976, is designed to encourage and reward business expansion through the acquisition of capital equipment.[14] The thrust of the credit is to accord tax breaks to businesses that invest heavily in new machinery and equipment. The more a firm invests, the more of a credit it gets against its tax bill. Thus, it paid for the Budd Corporation not just to spend a few million dollars fixing up their Philadelphia plant, but rather to spend much more building a brand-new plant in a rural location, since the increased investment triggered an increased tax credit that lowered their corporate tax bill.

The investment tax credit works to encourage new plants, not just modernization of existing plants, thus encouraging businesses to leave their urban plants entirely and strike out for a new location. Cities don't get their share of investment tax credit-generated business, since they cannot offer the large parcels of land and attractive new locations for manufacturing businesses. Cities have to try to persuade their manufacturing industry to stay and renovate their old plants in cities, a task made much harder by the investment tax credit. In fact, the whole orientation of the investment tax credit toward manufacturing is, in itself, antiurban. Cities are relying less and less on manufacturing and industry for their jobs and more and more on service businesses. Service firms don't have the kind of large capital needs that would enable them to use the investment tax credit to much effect. In New York City, for example, the number of manufacturing jobs dropped from 653,000 to 522,000 in just the three years between 1973 and 1976.[15] By rewarding industries with vast plant and equipment investment by the investment tax credit, the federal government accords them a form of aid that is denied to most urban business, which is primarily service-oriented in character. In the 1977 tax reform, Congress is taking a step to redress this imbalance through the enactment of a tax credit for new employment, but the long-standing bias in the tax law in favor of capital acquisition is hard to reverse.

One of the most interesting forms of discrimination against the urban and northern taxpayer is the failure of many federal deductions to recognize the impact of regional cost-of-living differences. Take, for example, the $750 allowed per person as the exemption on federal income tax forms—the most widely used deduction in the country. It should be obvious by now that $750 means a lot more in the South than it does in the North. A family of four in New York taking a $3,000 personal exemption can buy 34 percent *less* with its exemption than can a family in Dallas taking the same $3,000 exemption.

I was amazed to see broad-based liberal support for President Carter's tax "reform" which set one uniform level for the standard personal deduction permitted taxpayers who use the short form—that is, who do not itemize their deductions. Heretofore, the higher one's income, the higher the standard deduction one could take. At least this system helped out those using the short form who came from high cost-of-living areas. Their incomes may have been higher, but their permissible standard deduction was higher as well. But when Carter proposed that all taxpayers using the short form be permitted to take the same standard deduction—$3,000 for a family and $2,200 for an individual—he was assuring that regional cost-of-living differences would undermine the value of the deduction in the North and enhance it in the South.

I asked one congressman about the Carter proposal and explained how it would adversely affect his northeastern constituency. "That's a fascinating point," he said. "I don't think it has ever been brought out in the debate. Most liberals are for the Carter plan, since it would permit lower income people to have a higher deduction than they would get under the current system, but I don't think many of us would be for it if we realized that it would mean that the deduction our constituents could take would be worth less than that which the southern areas could take." I would, frankly, have been more impressed by his affirmation of my view had he acted upon the notion. The Carter proposal sailed through Congress without real liberal opposition and with a great deal of liberal—and northeastern—misguided support.[16]

There is nothing wrong with helping the poor by setting standard deductions, but let them be standardized within regions and adjusted among regions for cost-of-living differences. Until we learn to differentiate between tax relief to the poor and unfair tax advantages to those whose incomes appear to be lower because of their lower costs of living, we will fall into a trap wherein what liberals advocate as part of their economic ideology hurts their constituents in its economic effect. By indexing the income tax system for cost-of-living gaps we can accomplish the valid social objective of helping the poor while equalizing the treatment of different parts of America.

Actually, the theme of nonurban tax shelters runs throughout the tax law. All manner of special tax advantages are given businesses that locate in primarily rural areas and very few, if any, are given business in an urban locale. Farming, mining, oil, timber, are all richly rewarded and protected by tax benefits and tax shelters. But *urban* business is not given its share of the tax advantages and tax loopholes. This is not to say that urbanites don't invest in rural tax shelters. The rich in our cities can avail themselves of these tax shelters as easily as the rich anywhere in the country. But the businesses that are encouraged, the jobs that are created by these shelters, tend to be in rural areas. Among the poor and middle class, it is only the rural poor and the rural middle class that benefit from most tax shelters and the jobs they create.

To quantify this argument, I went through a list the federal government publishes of what it calls its "tax expenditures" (its tax benefits given special groups of people). The idea behind the listing is that these tax breaks are the same as a cash subsidy in that they result in a loss of federal tax revenues. There are about eighty tax expenditures listed, but most are not really more applicable to one region of the country than to another. But eighteen tax expenditures—worth about $17 billion in lost tax revenues—clearly benefit either the Northeast or the Sun Belt. As the following table indicates, the score: fourteen breaks worth $16.5 billion favor the Sun Belt and only four worth $600 million favor the Northeast.

TAX EXPENDITURES ORIENTED TO SUN BELT OR RURAL TAXPAYERS[17]

1. Supplements to salaries of military personnel, including provision of quarters and meals on military bases and quarters allowances for military families as well as a range of bonuses and special salary payments are exempt from taxation.
   - Since the overwhelming majority of military bases are located in the Sun Belt, this tax advantage is largely spent in proximity to southern areas.

     COST: $650 million
2. Farmers, including corporations engaged in agriculture, may deduct certain costs as current expenses, even though these expenditures were for inventories on hand at the end of the year or for capital improvements.
   - A tax benefit exclusively related to agriculture.

     COST: $475 million
3. Farm income derived from the sale of livestock, orchard, vineyards, and other agricultural activities is treated as capital gain rather than ordinary income.
   - A tax benefit exclusively related to agriculture.

     COST: $605 million
4. Capital costs necessary to bring a mineral deposit into production may, in certain instances, be deducted as current expenses rather than spread over the useful life of the property.
   - A tax benefit exclusively related to mining.

     COST: $1,035 million

5. Special depletion allowances for oil and other extractive industries.

- A tax benefit exclusively related to mining and other extractive industries such as oil.
COST: $1,595 million

6. Royalties from coal or iron ore deposits are treated as capital gains.

- A tax benefit exclusively conferred on the mining industry.
COST: $70 million

7. The gain on the cutting of timber is taxed at rates applicable to long-term capital gains, rather than at ordinary income rates.

- A tax benefit exclusively conferred on the lumber industry.
COST: $230 million

8. Deductability of state gasoline taxes.

- A tax benefit that accrues primarily to rural and suburban areas where auto use is far higher than in urban communities.
COST: $600 million

9. Depreciation on buildings other than rental housing in excess of straight line. Confers special tax advantages on homeowners.

- A tax benefit for homeowners which is, by definition, a primarily nonurban benefit, since urban housing, especially in the Northeast, tends to be heavily rental in character. (Depreciation on rental housing is listed as an urban benefit.)
COST: $215 million

10. Investment tax credit

- By rewarding capital investment in plant and equipment, this credit accrues primarily to the benefit of nonurban manufacturing and industry located in areas that have the physical space to accommodate such machinery.
COST: $1,445 million

11. Deferral of capital gains on home sales.

- Primarily, a benefit to homeowners who tend to be concentrated in nonurban areas.
  COST: $890 million

12. Deductability of mortgage interest on owner-occupied homes.
    - Of prime benefit to homeowners who are concentrated in nonurban areas, urban populations tending to be more likely to live in rental units.
      COST: $4,710 million
13. Deductability of property taxes on owner-occupied homes.
    - Of prime benefit to homeowners concentrated in nonurban areas, urban housing tending to be more rental in character.
      COST: $3,825 million
14. Credit for the purchase of new home.
    - Again, of prime benefit to homeowners.
      COST: $100 million
      TOTAL COST: $16,445 million

TAX EXPENDITURES ORIENTED TO NORTHEASTERN OR URBAN TAXPAYERS

1. Five-year amortization of housing rehabilitation costs.
   - Most renovation activity is primarily urban-oriented under this program.
     COST: $65 million
2. Tax credit for employing welfare recipients.
   - While not exclusively an urban program, its benefit goes primarily to urban areas which have a preponderance of welfare recipients.
     COST: $10 million
3. Exclusion of public assistance benefits from taxation.
   - Most P.A. recipients live in urban centers.
     COST: $130 million
4. Accelerated depreciation on rental housing.
   - Most rental housing is concentrated in urban communities.
     COST: $455 million
     TOTAL COST: $660 million

Let us not lose sight of one basic point: The residents of our cities are asked to bear a disproportionate share of the burden for supporting the federal government, a federal government we all have in common and for which all Americans bear an equal responsibility. Yet our equality at the ballot box is belied by our inequality at the Internal Revenue Service, an inequality not reflective of disproportionate wealth nor of the receipt of special benefit, but due instead to the accident of geographic residence.

Those who benefit from tax breaks don't live in cities. One need not discern an overt antiurban design in the pattern of deductions and credits permitted under the tax law. It is enough to say that the tax laws are written to benefit homeowners, corporate farmers, mining companies, capital intensive business, and a host of others whose common denominator is that they tend not to live in cities. The elderly, the poor, students, tenants, and mass-transit users do not attract similar legislative sympathy, and they happen to live in the cities.

9.

NO FEDERAL JOBS FOR THE NORTHEAST

The Federal Office Building in New York City is located at 1 Federal Plaza near New York's City Hall. It is a beautiful structure with fountains and, on any given summer day, dozens of people sunbathing on the benches and marble that decorate its plaza. But it is a curious sight to ride in its elevators. At least one elevator in each line in the building is coated with canvas to protect the elevator walls. One day I jokingly asked the attendant in the building's lobby if they kept up the canvas so that people, frustrated with federal bureaucracy, wouldn't hurt themselves banging their heads against the elevator walls. "No," he laughed, "that's not it, although maybe that's not a bad idea. We just keep them up because there are always so many offices moving in and out that it is a pain to keep putting the canvas up and taking it down every time somebody wants to move out some furniture."

His comment stayed with me when I examined data provided by the Bureau of Labor Statistics tracing the loss of jobs in New York City between 1969 and 1974. The bureau listed the industries that had experienced the greatest gains and the greatest losses in jobs during the four-year period. Near the top of the list of job losers was "federal government—11,000 jobs." With virtually no publicity, little protest, and no fanfare, the federal government had withdrawn 11,000 jobs from the New York economy! No wonder they had to put up canvas in the elevators, so federal agencies wouldn't damage their furniture as they fled New York City.

The federal government is not an equal opportunity employer, at least when it comes to providing jobs for Americans regardless of their geographic location. The federal government is a Sun Belt employer and one of that region's key sources of jobs. But precious few federal jobs find their way to the Northeast and its cities.

The geographic distribution of federal civilian employment reflects this sharp regional bias. As of June 30, 1975, the federal government employed 2,475,663 civilians, making it the largest employer in the country. But the Northeast got only 812,000 of these jobs.[1] Its fair per capita share is 1.1 million jobs. The Northeast gets 300,000 fewer federal jobs than is its fair per capita share.

FEDERAL CIVILIAN EMPLOYMENT, BY STATE[2]

Northeast			Sun Belt		
State	*% of U.S. Pop.*	*% of Federal Civilian Employment*	*State*	*% of U.S. Pop.*	*% of Federal Civilian Employment*
Connecticut	1.2	1.7	Alabama	1.7	2.1
Illinois	5.3	4.0	Arizona	.2	.6
Indiana	2.5	1.6	Arkansas	1.0	.7
Maine	.5	.5	California	9.9	11.1
Massachusetts	2.7	2.3	Georgia	2.3	2.8
Michigan	4.3	2.0	Florida	3.8	2.7
Minnesota	1.9	1.1	Louisiana	1.8	1.1
New Hampshire	.4	.2	Mississippi	1.1	.8
New Jersey	3.5	2.4	New Mexico	.5	1.0

Northeast			Sun Belt		
State	*% of U.S. Pop.*	*% of Federal Civilian Employment*	*State*	*% of U.S. Pop.*	*% of Federal Civilian Employment*
New York	8.6	6.5	North Carolina	2.5	1.5
Ohio	5.1	3.6	Oklahoma	1.3	2.0
Pennsylvania	5.6	5.2	South Carolina	1.3	1.1
Rhode Island	.4	.6	Tennessee	2.0	1.9
Vermont	.2	.1	Texas	5.7	5.5
Wisconsin	2.2	1.0	Virginia	2.3	2.8
TOTAL	44.4	32.8	TOTAL	37.4	37.7

The fifteen northeastern states receive only 32.8 percent of federal civilian jobs, although they comprise 44.4 percent of the nation's population.

There is no reason for this bias in federal employment. The Sun Belt is not somehow more related to the work for the federal government. Jobs provided by federal taxes should be distributed throughout the nation and not focused on any one area. To hear Ronald Reagan talk of the bloated federal bureaucracy, one would think he was talking about a strange and alien work force. In fact, he speaks of the jobs that help bolster his own state's economies.

The focus of federal employment has shifted increasingly in recent years away from the northeastern and Great Lakes states. Between 1960 and 1970, the number of federal employees grew by 24 percent. But federal civilian employment in New York, Pennsylvania, and New Jersey rose by only 1.3 percent during the same period. Overall, the growth in federal employment accrued almost entirely to the Sun Belt.

GROWTH IN FEDERAL CIVILIAN EMPLOYMENT, 1960-70[3]

Region	*% Growth in Federal Civilian Employment*
New England	3.5
Mid-Atlantic	1.3
East North Central	9.2
East South Central	14.7
South Atlantic	30.7
West South Central	21.0
TOTAL	24

Thus, in a ten-year period, about 5,000 federal jobs were added to the economies of New York, New Jersey, and Pennsylvania, whereas over 100,000 federal jobs were added to the economies of Virginia, North Carolina, South Carolina, Georgia, Florida, Mississippi, and Alabama.

Beyond the issues of equity inherent in this maldistribution of federal employment lies its real effect on the extent of unemployment in each of the northeastern states. If Michigan, for example, had the same proportion of federal employment as its share of the national population, the state would have 57,000 more jobs. More to the point, its unemployment rate, which stood at 6.6 percent in 1977, would now drop by 1.4 points to 5.4 percent—a lot lower than the national average.

It is surprising how many states could make significant dents in their joblessness rate by simply receiving their just share of federal employment.

CHANGE IN STATE UNEMPLOYMENT RATE IF IT RECEIVED THE SAME PROPORTION OF FEDERAL CIVILIAN EMPLOYEES AS IT HAS OF U.S. POPULATION[4]

State	*Civilian Labor Force (in thousands)*	*Additional Federal Jobs**	*Effect on Unemployment Rate*
Illinois	4,943	32,000	−0.6%
Indiana	2,385	22,284	−0.9%
Michigan	3,935	56,948	−1.4%
New Jersey	3,214	27,236	−0.8%
New York	7,549	51,996	−0.7%
Ohio	2,448	37,140	−1.5%
Wisconsin	2,082	29,712	−1.4%

**This column computes the additional federal jobs to which each state would be entitled if the distribution of such jobs were held in strict relationship to that state's share of the U.S. population. Thus, it indicates how many jobs Illinois would gain if it had 5.3 percent of total federal civilian employment—an amount equal to its percentage of national population—rather than the 4.0 percent of federal jobs it has at present.*

The effect of the antinortheastern pattern of federal employment is quite severe in many states. In three states—Ohio, Wisconsin, and Michigan—the unemployment rate could be brought down by about one and a half percentage points were these states simply to receive their fair per capita share of federal employment. Such an improvement in the employment prospects of the major northeastern states would, it seems to me, be far more direct an answer to our economic ills than the overall improvement of "business climate" upon which many seem to pin their hopes!

Here is the ultimate illustration of the need for justice in dealing with the problems of northern cities as opposed to giving them handouts. The National Conference of Mayors urged President Carter in their November 1976 meeting to promulgate a major program of public works jobs for America's cities. They pleaded that their high unemployment rates made such extraordinary aid necessary. But the evidence suggests that such "aid" is often not the key. What is needed is a fair apportionment of existing federal jobs and an end to the discriminatory antinortheastern bias in the allocation of these jobs: The cities need equity, not aid.

Some will challenge my contention that federal jobs are poorly apportioned among the states. They will argue that there is nothing inherently more just about apportioning federal employment on the basis of population than the current lack of any system for their distribution. In this chapter, I only use population as an indicator of the current maldistribution of these jobs and the undue emphasis on southern employment in the federal public sector. Actually, federal employment should, rationally, be allocated based on objective indices of need such as unemployment. When such an index is used, the higher unemployment rates of the northeastern states entitle them to an even greater share of federal employment than would seem to be warranted were just population used.

Taken together, the pattern of antinortheastern bias in federal employment and taxation constitutes a significant economic deprivation of all northeastern states and cities.

10.

THE PENTAGON: A FIVE-SIDED BUILDING THAT FACES SOUTH

When you walk through the streets of San Antonio, Texas, you cannot escape the feeling that it is a town under military occupation. Uniforms appear at every corner, in every store, and in every barbershop. The entire city seems to be invaded by a swarm of armed forces personnel. But San Antonio's military invasion has not brought with it devastation and disruption; rather, it has brought wealth and income to a city almost totally dependent on military bases, purchases, and contracts. San Antonio is a one-industry town: defense.

One dollar out of four earned in Bexar County (which contains San Antonio) comes from a defense budget—$428 million in military salaries and $407 million to civilian personnel employed by the Defense Department. The county contains Brooks Air Force Base, Goodfellow Air Force Base, Kelly Air Force Base, Randolf Air Force Base, and Fort Sam Houston. The Defense Department spends $1,500 a year in San Antonio for every man, woman, and child in the city. San Antonio has 756,000 people while New York City has 7.5 million, but San Antonio gets 50 percent more defense money than does the city of New York.[1]

The entire Sun Belt is incredibly dependent on defense dollars for its economic growth and survival. Without the defense budget, the Sun Belt simply could not sustain the economic boom of which it has boasted for the past decade. In all, almost 9 percent of the personal income of the fifteen Sun Belt states comes from the defense budget—nearly one dollar in ten. The entire economic superstructure of these states is dependent on defense spending.

It is interesting to examine the ratio of defense spending to personal income in the Northeast as opposed to the Sun Belt states:

DEFENSE EXPENDITURES AS PERCENTAGE OF PERSONAL INCOME[2]

Northeast		Sun Belt	
State	*% of Personal Income Attributable, Directly, to Defense Spending*	*State*	*% of Personal Income Attributable, Directly, to Defense Spending*
Connecticut	11.8	Alabama	8.1
Illinois	2.2	Arizona	12.6
Indiana	3.4	Arkansas	4.5
Maine	4.2	California	10.1
Massachusetts	6.6	Florida	7.3
Michigan	2.2	Georgia	8.5
Minnesota	2.7	Louisiana	6.1
New Hampshire	10.3	Mississippi	15.6
New Jersey	3.5	New Mexico	10.2
New York	3.8	North Carolina	6.7
Ohio	3.6	Oklahoma	8.2
Pennsylvania	3.9	Tennessee	3.6
Rhode Island	3.6	Texas	8.1
Vermont	9.1	Virginia	10.5
Wisconsin	1.6	South Carolina	10.3
TOTAL	3.8	TOTAL	8.8

While the defense budget contributes a negligible 3.8 percent of the personal income of the Northeast, it is responsible, directly, for 8.8 percent of income in the Sun Belt South. Six southern states are dependent on the defense budget for 10 percent or more of their personal income, including both California and Virginia, while only two northeastern states are so dependent. Only one southern state—Tennessee—depends on the defense budget for less than 4 percent of her personal income, while ten northeastern states have such minimal dependence on defense spending.

Those who would point to the business climate of the Sun Belt as a decisive factor in its economic growth would do well to ponder the extent to which the private enterprise boom in that region is actually merely a manifestation of public sector stimulation through defense appropriations.

The defense budget represents more than a commitment by the United States to a certain number of men and women in the armed forces and a certain amount of weaponry. It is a decision by the United States government to purchase over $100 billion a year of goods and services. The location of these expenditures is an absolutely vital decision on which the prosperity of much of the nation depends. While northern liberal Democrats tend to focus on issues of whether the defense budget represents the most fruitful of expenditures in terms of national priorities, Sun Belt congressmen look on the defense budget as a source of economic sustenance. Their concerns are often less with what is to be spent or at what price, but where the spending is to go.

The imbalance of the defense budget is just unbelievable. It is worth examining on a detailed, state-by-state basis:

DEFENSE ALLOCATIONS AND POPULATION COMPARED[3]

Northeast			Sun Belt		
State	*% Share of Defense Budget*	*% Share of National Pop.*	*State*	*% Share of Defense Budget*	*% Share of National Pop.*
Connecticut	3.2	1.5	Alabama	1.7	1.7
Illinois	1.9	5.3	Arizona	1.6	1.0
Indiana	1.6	2.5	Arkansas	0.5	1.0
Maine	0.2	0.5	California	17.2	9.9
Massachusetts	2.9	2.7	Florida	3.6	3.8

Northeast			Sun Belt		
State	*% Share of Defense Budget*	*% Share of National Pop.*	*State*	*% Share of Defense Budget*	*% Share of National Pop.*
Michigan	1.5	4.3	Georgia	2.6	2.3
Minnesota	0.8	1.9	Louisiana	1.5	1.8
New Hampshire	0.5	0.4	Mississippi	1.9	1.1
New Jersey	2.2	3.5	New Mexico	0.6	0.5
New York	5.9	8.6	North Carolina	2.2	2.5
Ohio	2.8	5.1	Oklahoma	1.4	1.3
Pennsylvania	3.4	5.6	South Carolina	1.5	1.3
Rhode Island	0.3	0.4	Tennessee	0.9	2.0
Vermont	0.2	0.2	Texas	6.9	5.7
Wisconsin	0.5	2.2	Virginia	5.4	2.3
TOTAL	27.9	44.7	TOTAL	49.5	38.2

Thus, the northeastern states, with 45 percent of America's people, get only 28 percent of the national defense spending while the states of the Sun Belt, with 38 percent of the population, get almost half of the national defense budget. It is not hard to understand the economic growth of southern California, for example, when one reflects on the fact that the state gets 17 percent of national defense spending, about three times the New York State allocation.

The southern and western bias in the national defense budget is certainly understandable in historic terms. The South has always been the most promilitary of the nation's regions, dating back to pre-Civil War days when the military was an integral part of the southern plantation culture. During the Vietnam War, for example, peace sentiment was far more shallow in the South than in any other part of the nation and loyalty to national defense policies ran deeper. The West had come by its share of the defense budget through a long emphasis on aerospace development stemming from the research efforts of the University of California. By taking the lead in national aerospace research, southern California has been able to lay claim to much of the national spending on military aviation and space technology.

But much of the emphasis on southern defense spending stems not from historical antecedents but from congressional politics. The Armed Services Committees of the House and Senate are traditionally the loci of military decision making in the Congress. Defense issues are often incredibly complex and the average member of Congress is loath to overrule those on the Armed Services Committees whose expertise and experience in the details of defense budgeting they are inclined to respect. Members of these committees are often privy to top-secret information which, while technically available to the other members of Congress, often takes too much time and background for noncommittee members to use or understand.

The reliance on the Armed Services Committees is especially pronounced in the House of Representatives. While it is possible for a Senator, with a substantial staff, to acquire some expertise in defense matters even if he is not on the Armed Services Committee, the average congressman, with fewer than twenty staffers, does not have the same capacity for acquiring a familiarity with defense issues. As a result, the thirty-nine members of the House Armed Services Committee have a decisive influence over the flow of defense funds and plans.

In 1975 I worked with Congresspeople Tom Downey, Bob Carr, and Pat Schroeder, liberal Democratic opponents of high defense spending in the preparation of their answer to the ambitious military spending programs of the Ford administration. It was clear, throughout, that efforts on the floor of the House of Representatives to overturn the approval of the defense budget by the Armed Services Committee were likely to fail. Congressman Joseph Addabbo of Queens, New York, one of the most effective opponents of excessive defense spending, told me that "floor fights on major weapons systems rarely succeed. Most members just follow what the Armed Services Committee decides and won't overrule it."

Due to their influence, the Pentagon works hard to court members of the House Armed Services Committee, spending a great deal of time lobbying the members, briefing them, and negotiating with them. The Pentagon long ago learned that one of the most effective ways to get a congressman to vote for defense spending was to locate some of it in the congressman's district. As a result, the members of the House Armed Services Committee, who represent districts in counties with 25 percent of America's population, are able to get 38 percent of the total defense budget in their districts.

Of the thirty-nine members of the House Armed Services Committee, twenty-three come from the South or the Sun Belt and none come from the cities of New York, Boston, Chicago, Philadelphia, Cleveland, or Minneapolis. In fact, only one northern member of the committee comes from a city with a population of 250,000 or more. It is no wonder that the Northeast fails to get its fair share of defense spending.

Why northern liberals choose to boycott the Armed Services Committee was brought home to me when I spoke with Congressman Theodore S. Weiss immediately after his election, in 1976, to fill the formidable vacancy left by Bella Abzug in the House of Representatives. When I recently asked Ted Weiss, a newly elected liberal, whether he would consider service on the Armed Services Committee, he was surprised by my suggestion and answered that he was considering a seat on the Banking and Housing or Education and Labor committees. He ultimately ended up on the Education and Labor Committee with many other northeastern members. A strong and early opponent of the war in Vietnam, Weiss would no more have considered service on the Armed Services Committee than he would have on the old House Un-American Activities Committee. This trend of thought is common among liberal northeastern congressmen. Opposed to major defense spending, they tacitly refuse to maximize the share of these monies, which could flow to their home districts. Even when a northern liberal ends up on the Armed Services Committee, he often finds himself cast more as an adversary of the defense budget than as a determiner of its geographic allocation. One northern liberal senator who sits on the Senate Armed Services Committee recently said that he did not want to fight to obtain more defense spending for his state because he did not want to be beholden to the Pentagon.

Most of us see the defense budget as part of an overall issue of national priorities and policy choices. We argue about whether funds should be allocated to bombers or day-care centers, missile systems or social services. Candidates for public office are often judged by their views concerning the relative priorities of military as opposed to social spending. Nevertheless, it seems to me that we must come to regard defense spending as a part of our national economy. Whether or not we approve of the continued allocation of almost a tenth of our gross national product to military operations, if we fail to get our regional share of this money, we sacrifice much of our economic potential and, along with it, much of our ability to gratify our more idealistic social impulses. This may be more expedient than idealistic, but such are the compromises economic reality imposes. Gesture politics does not feed, clothe, and house people.

The economic stagnation of the Northeast, a concomitant result of federal spending patterns, has caused budget cuts far more severe in their effect on social services than even those that resulted from the reduction in federal spending under the Nixon and Ford administrations. New York City, for example, survived the cutbacks in federal social spending between 1968 and 1974 without finding it necessary to cut government employment or service delivery. Only when local tax revenues began to dry up during the recession of 1974-75 and its traumatic aftermath for the Northeast were major decreases in services and city employment necessary.

A recent issue of *New York Affairs,* a quarterly publication of the Institute for the Study of the City, ran a cover with the headline "Unemployment: The Number One Urban Problem." Gradually, we are coming to realize that without a sound economic base, it is absurd to imagine that we can make progress in improving the quality of life of the poor or in upgrading our society's human services. If economic stagnation and joblessness are our major urban problems, should we not try to tap the economic benefits of military allocations? Obviously, it would benefit Harlem more to get federal day-care dollars than federal defense dollars. But, equally obviously, it is of more benefit to Harlem that it get federal defense dollars than that it get nothing.

Indeed, almost alone among northern liberals, New York's Senator Daniel Patrick Moynihan seems to appreciate the importance of generating a greater share of the defense budget for the Northeast. I spoke with him during his race for the Senate in 1976 and we discussed my data concerning the shortchanging of the Northeast by the federal budget. "It is really the hard areas—defense, contracts, procurement—where the Northeast loses out. In the soft areas—welfare, Medicaid, and so forth—areas which don't help you build the economy, we do all right. In a sense, we get the aid we need to stay alive, but not the contracts we need to grow."[4] I was impressed with the distinction Moynihan drew between hard and soft aid. It is unfortunate that the overwhelming efforts of those who represent us in Congress go toward generating "soft" aid through service on the Education and Labor Committee or the Interstate Commerce and Health Committee of the House rather than to "hard" spending through work on defense.

I discussed the problems of the imbalance in the defense budget at a meeting of union organizers from the International Union of Electrical Workers in Columbus, Ohio, where I had been asked to speak on the problems of the Northeast. The union, whose members work on a great many defense projects, was concerned about the imbalance in Pentagon funds. One of the audience pinned me down with the question "Doesn't the orientation to the Sun Belt in defense spending reflect the edge that region has in defense technology? Could you even find a firm in New York City which could handle a contract to design a new type of rocket or missile?"

The question is well taken, but it has its answers. One of them was given me a few weeks later by the campaign manager of a southern client who is running for the Senate. We were discussing the imbalance in federal spending and he agreed that the Northeast was getting less than its share. "In fact," he said, "we now have to reverse what we used to do. We used to see to it that the South got the cream of defense money, for example, to help the region build and grow economically. Maybe now we have to reverse the trend and start giving the growth industries to the North."

The point is that the South did not develop its defense industrial capability through its own efforts. Defense industry was dumped into its lap by federal research and development contracts. It was Washington, through the defense contracts themselves, that stimulated the growth of a defense industry in the South. Defense was not like cotton or tobacco, a native southern commodity. It was brought there by federal policy, and it can now, by the same token, be shared with the rest of America through federal policy. In awarding contracts for such defense work, undoubtedly the lack of a long history of defense contracting places many northeastern locales at a disadvantage. Their industry may simply lack the technological capacity for most next-generation defense work. At best this failure may add to the cost of a bid filed with the Defense Department; at worst it may place many kinds of defense work beyond the reach of northern and urban firms.

Defenders of the defense budget's southern bias may argue that it makes little sense to add to the cost of weapons systems by contracting with firms without established track records or ongoing facilities capable of ready adaptation to the production requirements of the new system. But continued adherence to this policy will dictate that future contractual awards go to the companies that now dominate the field, continuing the grievous economic consequences for the rest of the nation. Only by recognizing that it is in the national interest that so major a portion of federal activity as the defense budget not be so slanted to the benefit of one region will we overcome this vicious cycle. The Pentagon must come to consider the need for regional balance in its contracting alongside such factors as technical capacity and cost in awarding its work. Such a policy will not be new for the Pentagon. The Lockheed Corporation, for example, has been kept afloat through the seventies by generous federal loans. The theory behind this financing is that it was in the national interest to maintain a vigorous military-industrial capacity and to assure the survival of major defense contractors. It is surely not too great a conceptual leap to say that as long as we continue to spend a tenth of our national wealth on defense, we should not undermine the economy of half of America by refusing it a rightful share of this money. The defense budget is, after all, financed by taxes collected from the entire country. Indeed, these taxes actually fall more heavily on those in the Northeast and Great Lakes states. To extract wealth with one hand through taxation and not replenish it with the other through spending is to set in motion an economic contraction. Such cramps are not in the national interest.

But the defense budget is not all composed of high-technology contracts and complex research and development. Well over half of the total defense budget goes for manpower salaries. In fact, the Defense Department employs about as many *civilians*—excluding military personnel—than all other federal agencies except the Postal Service combined. But the bias of the defense spending patterns toward the Sun Belt is clearly illustrated in the distribution of military installations and bases throughout the country. The greatest number of such bases are located in the fifteen states of the Sun Belt. In fact, of 440 major military bases and installations in the fifty states, 234, more than half, are in the fifteen states of the Sun Belt South. Only 90 are in the fifteen northeastern-Great Lakes states.

DEFENSE INSTALLATIONS BY STATE[5]

Northeast		Sun Belt	
State	*Number of Bases*	*State*	*Number of Bases*
Connecticut	3	Alabama	7
Illinois	11	Arizona	7
Indiana	5	Arkansas	3
Maine	7	California	70
Massachusetts	7	Florida	30
Michigan	6	Georgia	12

Northeast		Sun Belt	
State	*Number of Bases*	*State*	*Number of Bases*
Minnesota	4	Louisiana	5
New Hampshire	2	Mississippi	4
New Jersey	9	North Carolina	12
New York	11	Oklahoma	6
Ohio	5	South Carolina	15
Pennsylvania	15	Tennessee	5
Rhode Island	3	Texas	21
Vermont	1	Virginia	32
Wisconsin	1	New Mexico	5
TOTAL	90	TOTAL	234

California has 70 installations, Virginia has 32, Texas 21, but New York has only 11 and Ohio 5. This overwhelming Sun Belt predominance in military installations carries with it substantial economic advantages. Not only does federal defense money flow directly to the uniformed men and women at such bases, a substantial amount of federal civilian employment comes along with military installations. Even when military installations are located in northern states, they are not near or in large cities. Of the 90 bases in the Northeast, only 23 are near large urban centers, whereas of the 234 southern bases, 95 are in or near sizable urban areas. There is no rationale for this heavy southern bias in the location of military installations. There are no guarantees that wars will only be fought in tropical climates nor is there any shortage of suitable accomodations for such installations in the Northeastern area.

The Northeast's inability to garner a more generous share of defense spending not only sacrifices a certain amount of federal spending, employment, and purchasing orders, northeastern industry also sacrifices its ability to take part in a host of enterprises that are direct spin-offs of military work. As more of the defense budget becomes centered around sophisticated computer technology, communications systems, aerospace development, and modern electronics, the defense contracts awarded to the Sun Belt confer upon that region an important advantage in a wide variety of civilian areas, as indirect but related benefits.

When, for example, a firm is awarded a contract for production of the guidance system of a Phoenix missile, it must acquire an expertise in miniature computerization that gives it a vital edge in commercial sales. Those industries that specialize in production of military aircraft obviously enjoy an important advantage in the technology essential for commercial flying as well. When the Defense Department contracted for uniforms, guns, tanks, and more mundane hardware in earlier years, it was not clear that such allocations conferred a significant economic advantage in the competition for civilian work. The current high-technology defense contracting amounts to nothing less than a federally subsidized head start in seeking an array of nondefense work. One need only consider the mounting arms trade throughout the globe to trace the advantage that goes with federal defense contracts. Dozens of major American manufacturers regularly supplement their sales to the Defense Department with orders from foreign military customers. In all but a handful of instances, the Sun Belt states have a decided edge in this competition because of their head start in military work achieved through federal contracts.

Therefore, when the federal government contracts with the McDonnell-Douglas Corporation for the research, development, and production of the F-15 plane, it subsidizes and finances the Missouri firm's entrance into an important new area of foreign trade as well as of domestic defense production. The McDonnell-Douglas firm has now realized important successes in the sale of its plane to Israel, and its contemplated sale to Saudi Arabia, an important boon to the Missouri economy.

As we noted in the discussion of the energy crisis, the ability to produce defense commodities in which the Arab world is vitally interested has helped give the Sun Belt an edge in attracting oil dollars back into the United States after they have flowed out of our country to the rulers of the Arab world. This advantage in world trade is merely symptomatic of the host of advantages that accrue to the South which stem from its lead in defense research—a lead to which the federal government has staked the Sun Belt through the bias in its own defense spending policies.

Obviously, it is impossible in the limited confines of this work to analyze fully the reasons for the heavy southern bias of the defense budget. It stems in part from the dogged determination with which the region's congressional representatives pursue federal spending. Obviously, the warm climates of Florida and Texas give them certain advantages in the competition for defense installations. Other factors, such as the zeal with which the University of California promoted aerospace research in the fifties and sixties, are now paying off in defense spending.

We must stop looking at the defense budget in purely military terms. On the one hand, the Pentagon should no longer base its decision on the locale of defense spending purely on military or political considerations. On the other hand, liberals must not treat defense money as some sort of pariah to be avoided at all costs. If we eschew defense spending in the Northeast because it is antiliberal or immoral and if the federal government continues to allocate defense spending to its traditional southern locale, the entire national economy will suffer. Although Congress may debate for months the precise amount of deficit spending that would be useful for the economy, if our legislators continue to pay almost no attention to the proper distribution of defense spending, all efforts at economic balancing will prove self-defeating by according too much stimulation to one region and not enough to another. We must not have a regional defense budget, but a national military spending program. The monies spent wisely and distributed with care not only can protect us against attack from abroad but can help inoculate the economy from its peculiar internal vulnerabilities.

11.

HOW WASHINGTON PAYS THE NORTHEAST IN CONFEDERATE MONEY

A friend of mine worked for the State Department giving lectures in a variety of foreign countries. His basic salary and fee structure for the lectures was uniform, but he was given a different per diem living allowance in each country to which he went. When he lectured in Santiago, Chile, he was given one sum to live off but a different sum in Caracas, Buenos Aires, and in European cities. His duties were the same and he was expected to live at the same standard of living in each place, but the State Department knew that living costs varied in each part of the world and that it must vary the living allowance it gave its employees so that they could adjust for the different prices in each area.

The Atlantic Richfield Company does the same thing in this country.[1] When one of its executive workers moves from Atlanta to New York, he gets a 20 percent pay hike just to account for cost-of-living differences. His extra pay is not seen as an increase in salary, just an adjustment in salary to take account of the higher living costs in New York. Metropolitan Life Insurance Company varies the pay of many of its employees depending on the cost of living in the area in which they live.[2]

Whenever I shop at the A&P in my neighborhood, I think of the State Department, Atlantic Richfield, and Metropolitan Life. Why can't we pay our old people and our food stamp recipients the same way these corporations and agencies pay their employees? More times than I care to count, I have stood on line behind a senior citizen and watched him count out painfully his change to pay for some junk food like Hamburger Helper or phony mashed potatoes because he cannot afford to feed himself real food. I've often thought about how little the food stamps of a person on line with me will really buy at the high price levels that prevail in New York.

When I was in Atlanta working on this book, I spoke with a number of experts on the problems of the elderly. Their unanimous view was that the elderly in Atlanta had an easier time of it than those up North because, in the words of one expert, "their social security checks go further here." Costs are lower in other parts of the country, so why do we pay the elderly, veterans, disabled, and poor in the high cost-of-living areas of the Northeast the same amount of money as we pay them in the lower cost-of-living areas? Why can't America pay her veterans, elderly, and disabled in the same way as corporations pay their executives and the government pays its diplomats—differently in different regions to correspond to different costs of living?

This federal blind spot in failing to skew its payments to the elderly and poor to adjust for regional costs of living is a key cause of our regional economic malaise. We in the Northeast, by getting the same-size federal checks as those in other parts of the country, are getting less in *real* dollars than do people in other areas. The result is that our economy receives less of a stimulus from these payments than would be the case were they adjusted for cost-of-living differences. This is especially significant when one examines the historical context of these payments to the poor and elderly. The money the government pays to its poor through nine different programs is lumped under the economic term "cash transfer payments." These programs include:

Retirement insurance (Social Security)
Disability insurance (Social Security)
Survivor's insurance (Social Security)
Supplementary security income (SSI)
Food stamps
Veterans' benefits
Earned income tax credit
Railroad retirement benefits
Military retired pay

Together, these programs provide $115.1 billion to American citizens, a sum equal to almost 10 percent of total personal income in the country.[3] Cash transfers flow to the poorest elements of the population, people who do not deposit their checks in savings accounts, but who go out and spend the money on the necessities of life. As a result, the economic effect of giving them these payments is most positive because they set in motion a chain reaction of spending which helps the economy develop and prosper. In fact, these cash transfers are seen by economists as a way of helping a country recover from a recession. Thus, as more people are out of work, more get cash transfer payments, and this in turn causes more people to spend money and get the economy out of its slump again. This type of aid is called "countercyclical" by economists–whenever the cycle turns up, cash transfer payments drop as more people find work.

But when the Northeast is paid these cash transfers in absolute dollars instead of real dollars, in dollars that do not adjust for regional cost-of-living differences as opposed to those that do, the countercyclical effect of this aid is vastly reduced. Less money is pumped into the ailing economies of the Northeast and less is available to help counter the recession.

SOCIAL SECURITY

The single largest cash transfer payment program is Social Security, paying out over $80 billion in annual benefits.[4] Enacted in 1937, the Social Security system is the cornerstone of the New Deal programs of the Roosevelt administration. It is based on the principle that special payroll taxes on the employed population finances benefits for those who are retired and had contributed to the system during their working years.

Social Security has become the mainstay of existence for millions of elderly, disabled, and widowed people throughout the nation. Its monthly payments, though not generous, provide a basic sustenance for millions who have no other source of income. Unfortunately, the checks sent to people in different regions of the country are not adjusted to take account of the different costs of living in each area. Elderly people who are similarly situated have worked for the same period at the same wage, receive the same check each month. Despite the surface equity of such a plan, regional differences in living costs make the system, in fact, quite discriminatory against those who live in high living-cost areas like the Northeast.

The Bureau of Labor Statistics of the federal government publishes data each year on the cost of living for a retired couple in different parts of the nation. One is struck by the huge variations in living costs in urban as opposed to rural and in northern as opposed to southern areas. The Social Security system's failure to adjust for these differences in their payment schedules means, of course, that the *real* worth of a Social Security check is greater in the South than in the North.

LIVING COSTS FOR A RETIRED COUPLE[5]
Northern (New York) vs. Southern (Dallas)
Urban vs. Rural

Expenditure Category	*New York*	*Dallas*	*Urban*	*Rural*
Food at home	$1,581	$1,271	$1,445	$1,406
Food away from home	175	130	241	160
Renter costs	1,607	1,121	1,368	1,010
Homeowner costs	1,912	905	1,275	901
Home furnishings and operation	758	606	679	457
Transportation	344	504	469	439
Clothing	302	287	310	272
Other family consumption	316	283	299	210
Other items	539	454	800	727
TOTAL BUDGET	$6,353*	$5,025*	$5,637*	$4,746*

**Numbers do not add up, since not all people incur all expenses.*

I only wish that the Social Security Administration would read the data furnished by the Bureau of Labor Statistics. While with the one hand, the Social Security Administration is sending out checks to America's elderly of equal amount, regardless of where they live, with the other, the Bureau of Labor Statistics is publishing data that suggests that it costs 25 percent more to live as an elderly couple in New York than in Dallas and about 20 percent more to live in a city than in a rural community.

The implication is simple: When the city resident opens his or her Social Security envelope, the check will mean less in terms of food, clothing, shelter, and transportation than it will when opened in a southern city. In a very real sense, the northern Social Security recipient is paid in a different currency than is the southerner. It is a currency worth far less and able to buy much less, a currency debased by more rampant and continuing inflation. In a sense, it is now the northerner who is paid in Confederate money.

The failure of the Social Security system to adjust for cost-of-living disparities creates a form of built-in economic discrimination against the Northeast in the distribution of over $80 billion in annual benefits. The fifteen states of the Northeast and Great Lakes regions collected $29,441 million in fiscal 1975 from survivors, disability, and old age Social Security benefits.[6] According to the Bureau of Labor Statistics, living costs in the northeastern area run an average of 9 percent above the national average.[7] If the Social Security payments made to these states reflected their higher living costs and if payments were equalized in *real* value, the states of the northeastern region would stand to gain over $2.5 billion in increased Social Security payments alone, an amount likely to prove quite significant in its economic impact.

Ironically, while the Social Security system fails to recognize regional differences in the cost of living in its payment of benefits, it exploits these very differences in the collection of its revenues. The Social Security tax system currently requires employer and employee each to contribute 5.85 percent of the first $16,500 of an employee's income. If the employee earns less than $16,500, he and his employer must each pay 5.85 percent of his total income; if he earns more, only the first $16,500 of his income is taxed.

Just as with the income tax, such a tax system is clearly discriminatory against high cost-of-living areas. A northerner may earn $16,500 and thus pay a tax of $965 while a southerner may earn $14,000 and pay only a tax of $819. Yet each may have an identical standard of living. It would simply cost fewer dollars to achieve the same living standard in the South as in the North and hence lead to the payment of less in the way of Social Security taxes.

Especially when one considers that the Social Security tax is paid not only by employee but by employers as well, the devastating impact of this failure to adjust the tax level for regional cost-of-living differences becomes apparent. A northern employer is penalized for his location in a high cost-of-living area. He must pay his employees more money than he would in the South to compensate for the higher cost of living here, and then he is obliged to pay 5.85 percent of that higher wage in Social Security taxes. Were he to move his plant to the South, the employer could cut his wage payments and cut his Social Security tax payments as a result, without calling on his employees to cut their life-styles or living standard.

Curiously, the Social Security system once *did* take account of cost-of-living differences in its tax structure but stopped doing so as an indirect result of *liberal* pressure from northern congressional Democrats. In 1973 the Social Security tax rate stood at 5.85 percent—as it is today—but that tax rate was levied only on the first $10,500 of an employee's income. The Congress faced a choice: It could raise the 5.85 percent rate or it could tax more than just the first $10,500 of income. It chose to raise the income level rather than the tax rate because it was fairer to the poor. Congress—at the urging of liberal members—was asked not to tax the poor more, but to raise the ceiling on the Social Security tax, thereby making higher-income workers pay more in taxes.

The approach seems fair on the surface: Make higher-income workers pay Social Security taxes on more of their income rather than asking everybody to pay more regardless of how much money they earn. Unfortunately, the Congress failed to distinguish between those who were genuinely low income (poor) or simply had low incomes because they lived in a low cost-of-living area.

As long as the Social Security tax was levied only on a relative low level of wages, it adjusted, in effect, for regional cost-of-living disparities. One may have earned $16,000 in New York only to achieve the same buying power and standard of living as a $13,000 income in Mississippi, but the Social Security tax was only levied on the first $10,500 of each income. The actual amount of money paid into the system by each taxpayer would be equal, since the Social Security tax is levied *only* on the first $10,500 of the New Yorker's and the Mississippian's income. The fact that the New Yorker's income was higher than the Mississippian's made no difference.

Nevertheless, when the tax base was raised to $16,500, much more of the average employee's income was suddenly made subject to Social Security taxes. For a large part of the nation's population, the Social Security tax base now exceeded their total wage income, thereby rendering their entire income subject to the Social Security tax rate in contrast to only a portion of it, as had been the case under the lower tax base.

Thus, the inherent differences in wage rates between the northeastern cities, with their high costs of living, and the Sun Belt areas, with their lower costs, could begin to register on the distribution of the Social Security tax burden. The net result of this system is to create vast inequities in the Social Security tax burdens of each state. New York State, for example, with 8.6 percent of the country's population, paid 11 percent of the nation's Social Security taxes in 1973.[8]

The anomaly of the Social Security system stands out starkly: Those who live in high cost-of-living areas must expect to pay more in Social Security taxes but receive no more in benefits to compensate for their higher cost of living. What an anomaly that a program developed by a former governor of New York State, Franklin Delano Roosevelt, should be so injurious to the Northeast and so shortchange its elderly. Of course, Roosevelt could not have foreseen how living-cost differences would diminish the Social Security check his Hyde Park neighbors would receive while augmenting the value of the checks his Warm Springs neighbors would get.

FOOD STAMPS

During the 1977 blackout in New York City, I was walking in lower Manhattan near my home when I overheard two black women in worried conversation. The power blackout had left all New York refrigerators sickeningly warm on that humid, muggy night and food spoilage seemed inevitable. But the problems of food preservation assumed a new dimension for me when I heard one of the women say to the other, "And it's two days before food stamp time, I don't know how I am going to replace the food in my refrigerator."

Food stamps provide millions of Americans with their only chance at a decent diet. A program designed for all low-income people, whether employed or not, food stamps may be purchased by eligible recipients at a lower price than their face value. Thus, a person might buy $80 worth of food stamps for $55, the $25 subsidy representing the "bonus value" of the stamps. These stamps can then be used as cash for the purchase of food at any local store.

The Food Stamp Program is generally seen as a welfare program primarily for northern cities and their poor. In 1976 I flew back from Washington with a client, Congressman Fred W. Richmond of New York, and we were discussing the food stamp system. Richmond, now chairman of the House Subcommittee on Domestic Marketing, Consumer Relations, and Nutrition, is a leading congressional authority on food stamps. I mentioned to Richmond that New York State was badly shortchanged by the Food Stamp Program. I told him that New York had 8.6 percent of the nation's population, but got only 4.6 percent of the country's food stamp allocations. Richmond disagreed vigorously and said that my numbers had to be wrong. He contended that food stamps were an urban program and that New York was one of the major beneficiaries of the system. We bet a dollar over who was right and, on returning to his office, I proved that my data was correct.

Richmond was really shocked. He explained that the Agriculture Committee, on which he sat, had always considered the Food Stamp Program as the committee's "urban" program and had not realized that northern cities got so little from the program. Indeed, as the following data indicates, northern states benefit much less than southern areas from the Food Stamp Program.

AVERAGE ANNUAL FOOD STAMP BONUS VALUE, BY STATE[9]

Northeast		Sun Belt	
State	*Bonus Value*	*State*	*Bonus Value*
Connecticut	182.55	Alabama	261.83
Illinois	248.71	Arizona	245.56
Indiana	230.55	Arkansas	279.98
Maine	204.56	California	237.81
Massachusetts	145.94	Florida	269.28
Michigan	179.99	Georgia	227.23
Minnesota	210.98	Louisiana	295.04

Northeast		Sun Belt	
State	*Bonus Value*	*State*	*Bonus Value*
New Hampshire	170.84	Mississippi	281.28
New Jersey	221.74	New Mexico	300.90
New York	150.12	North Carolina	227.14
Ohio	274.25	Oklahoma	205.44
Pennsylvania	195.80	South Carolina	288.06
Rhode Island	172.47	Tennessee	265.45
Vermont	203.41	Texas	290.45
Wisconsin	179.99	Virginia	215.51
TOTAL	189.87	TOTAL	259.64

The Food Stamp Program thus awards the southern recipient about 25 percent more in extra food than the northern recipient. The reason for this disparity goes right back to the problem of high as opposed to low living-cost areas. Eligibility for food stamps is computed based upon income. The more one earns, the fewer food stamps he is entitled to receive. The northern poor may be just as hungry, just as destitute, and just as needy as the southern poor, but they have higher dollar incomes because their costs are higher. The northern poor must pay more for food, housing, transportation, and clothing than the southern poor, so they need higher incomes just to stay even. But the more money they earn, the fewer food stamps they may receive.

Oddly enough, the higher northern welfare benefits play a role in cutting the food stamp allotments to which the northern poor are entitled. Because northern welfare benefits are more liberal than southern benefits tend to be, the northern poor are entitled to fewer food stamps. How ironic that the northern state is punished for laying out more money for welfare by being denied federal aid for food stamps as a result, while the southern state is rewarded for shortchanging its poor by more federal food stamp aid.

Unfortunately, even if the northern and southern food stamp beneficiaries received identical allotments, the southerners' food stamps would go further since food costs more in the North than in the South. It is interesting to examine the Bureau of Labor Statistics data that outlines the extent of variation in northern and southern food prices.

FOOD COST DIFFERENCES AMONG AREAS OF THE NATION[10]
(for lower-income family)

Northeast		Sun Belt	
City	*Food Costs*	*City*	*Food Costs*
New York	$3,087	Baton Rouge	$2,657
Philadelphia	2,974	Atlanta	2,646
Boston	2,883	Houston	2,637
Chicago	2,842	Dallas	2,482
Pittsburgh	2,802	Austin	2,451
Detroit	2,833	Los Angeles	2,715
Milwaukee	2,814	San Diego	2,671
Cincinnati	2,805	Bakersfield	2,603
Minneapolis	2,707	Nashville	2,527
Indianapolis	2,689	Orlando	2,516

It is no wonder my neighbors on the night of the blackout were concerned that they had two full days until food stamps came out. There is no question that, although food stamps may be adequate in the South to satisfy basic food needs of the poor, they are hopelessly inadequate in the North because of the inbuilt bias of the program against high cost-of-living areas and states with generous welfare programs.

Indeed almost all federal cash transfer programs do not take any account of regional cost-of-living differences. The elderly in one part of the nation get more in real Social Security benefits than the elderly in another part. The southern veterans can buy more with their checks than can the northern veterans. Food stamps go further in the South than in the North. These inequities cost the Northeast and its poor, elderly, and veterans billions of dollars a year. By the simple act of closing its eyes to the existence of regional cost-of-living differences, the federal government compensates its poor, elderly, and veterans according to totally different economic scales in the North and in the South.

The individual injustice of these different payment levels is obvious. Are some veterans who have lost an arm more deserving than others by reason of their geographic location? Surely, there is a clear need to "index" these cash transfer payments so that each takes account of the purchasing power of the dollar in the community to which the check is being sent. Indexing is far from an alien principle. Atlantic Richfield, Metropolitan Life, and the State Department do it; one is hard pressed to understand why the Social Security Administration, the Veterans Administration, and the Food Stamp Program do not.

Only by sending unequal checks to different parts of the nation can we be sure that we are compensating our citizens equally. This anomaly is an economic fact of life in an atmosphere of different costs of living in different regions. Some reject such indexing schemes on the grounds that they serve to perpetuate cost-of-living differences. As we have explored earlier in this book, cost-of-living differences are not simply willed into existence, but are created by federal energy and food regulatory policies. It is by ending these policies and adjusting their economic impact that we can begin to level out living costs in America. Until we make progress on this score, it seems to me imperative that we not punish innocent people in high cost-of-living areas by paying them without opening our eyes to the very real and large differences in the worth and value of the dollar in different areas of the United States.

The consequences for cities of this federal policy of refusing to vary cash transfer payments to conform to cost-of-living variations are especially severe. Increasingly, the American city is becoming inhabited by the young, the old, and the poor, each a population uniquely dependent on cash transfer payments for survival. Between 1970 and 1974, for example, the population of New York City declined by 4.1 percent while the population aged sixty-five and over *increased* by 3.8 percent and the minority group population *rose* by 8 percent. By contrast, the number of people aged thirty-five to forty-four, the most self-supporting and productive group in the population, dropped by 16 percent in four years.[11]

As cities become increasingly populated by the elderly and the poor, their dependence on cash transfers from the federal government for their municipal economic survival increases. But at the very same time that the number of those in need of cash transfers in the cities *increased,* the real value of the cash transfers they received *decreased* relative to those of the rest of the nation in the face of the rising urban cost of living. By failing to adjust cash transfers for cost-of-living increases in each region of the nation, the federal government aims a blow at the most vulnerable part of a city's economy: its poor and its elderly. By denying them an adequate sustenance, the federal government erodes the buying power of city consumers, particularly in poor neighborhoods, and sets in motion a chain reaction that leads to more unemployment, crime, and social blight.

12.

HOW THE NORTHEAST GETS CHEATED BY FEDERAL AID PROGRAMS

Nineteen seventy-five was a tough year in Ohio politics. The state's newly elected Republican governor, James Rhodes, was locked in a head-to-head battle with the newly elected liberal Democratic lieutenant governor, Richard Celeste. The issue: Should Ohio spend more on social services to the poor and thereby use all the federal matching funds that were available? The federal government had set the preconditions of this struggle when it voted $2.5 billion under Title XX of the Social Security Act in 1975 for social service programs in the fifty states. Each state was entitled to receive 50 percent federal reimbursement for all of its social services spending up to a ceiling that related to that state's share of the national population. Under the program, Ohio was to get $126 million, but only if it spent $126 million itself on social services. Rhodes refused to spend that much and Celeste attacked him for wasting federal money.

I had a ringside seat for the battle that ensued, since I had worked closely with Celeste on programs and issues during his first year in office. I couldn't believe that Ohio was trying to decide whether to use all the social service aid Washington had earmarked for the state. In New York the social services aid program was also the subject of bitter debate between advocates of greater social services for children and the mayor of New York, Abraham D. Beame. The subject of the New York debate: Should New York City, having already exhausted all federal aid to which the social services formula entitled it, spend money on services to the poor *over and above* that which would be matched by the federal government with the understanding that the city would have to go it alone?

The contrast between these two discussions brought home to me very vividly the inequities of the federal grant and aid programs to the states. Some states are awarded so little in federal money relative to the services they provide their citizens and the problems they face that federal funds are totally inadequate while other states struggle to spend all the federal funds to which they are entitled.

Federal grants to the states have grown rapidly as a part of the federal budget. In 1950 these grants accounted for only 10 percent of all state and local government spending while today they have risen to 23 percent.[1] As the New Deal heritage altered government's attitude toward the social and economic needs of the average citizen, a greater impetus developed to use federal funds to supplement the largely inadequate resources of states and cities. Historical prejudice against excessive federal government involvement in the day-to-day affairs of the nation's communities militated against direct federal programs and in favor of grants by Washington to cities and states for local programs. At first, these grants in aid were usually given on a matching basis. For each dollar a state or city spent on a given program, the federal government would put up a sum of money to match it. A wide array of federal programs emerged for reimbursement to states until the national government began to become the world's largest foundation, distributing $60.5 billion in 1977 in grants to states and localities for purposes ranging from school bus driver training to the education of migrant workers' children.[2]

Cities in the Northeast found such federal grant programs a bonanza during the sixties. Anxious to meet the social needs of their citizens, northeastern cities eagerly responded to federal offers of reimbursement by launching ambitious social programs. Between 1965 and 1970, federal aid to New York City, for example, jumped from $264 million to $1,316 million, an increase of over 80 percent a year![3] The federal aid encouraged New York City and other localities to make greater and greater commitments for new social programs. Drug addiction treatment, day care, job training, vocational education, and a host of new programs were instituted in cities across America responding to the flow of federal funding.

But as the Nixon administration took office and the national tide of opinion veered to the right, discontent with liberal urban social spending began to be manifest in the White House and the Congress. Concern developed that matching programs were essentially open-ended invitations to spend money with the certain knowledge that federal reimbursement would be on the way. This animosity to rapid increases in urban spending manifested itself in a thorough recasting of many major federal aid programs to deviate from the matching formula mold by placing a ceiling on total federal reimbursement and forcing all localities and states to live within it. Unfortunately, states and cities throughout the Northeast had already launched their social programs, encouraged by the seemingly endless flow of federal aid that had been manifest during the Johnson administration. Suddenly cut off from this federal aid, cities were left to flounder, or in the phrase of the era, to twist slowly in the wind.

New York City Comptroller Harrison J. Goldin described this transformation in federal policies: "During that period [the sixties], New York, with its customary social commitment, tooled up to an extent unparalleled by others to meet the challenge and match the grants adding thousands of employees and, pursuant to Federal incentive, locking in a broad and expensive service delivery system. Today, we are left with the costs of that war but without the consolation of victories. We are also left with a superstructure of public service responsibilities grown too heavy for its foundation of local revenue sources."[4]

Thus, federal aid to New York City, which had grown by 80 percent a year during the late sixties, grew by only 11 percent a year between 1970 and 1974.[5] New York and other urban centers were left adrift. They had committed themselves to social programs, but now found the rug pulled out from under them by the Nixon and Ford administrations' alterations in federal aid programs. Washington had changed signals, but the states and cities of the Northeast could not simply will away the hopes and expectations the programs of the sixties had left in their wake.

The Nixon-Ford formulae have a curious superficial fairness and equity to them. On face value, they seem to be rational and reasonable methods of allocating federal aid and resources. But a close examination of their thrust and direction as well as of the fine print leads inevitably to the conclusion that they are terribly unfair and have left America's cities holding the bag. These formulae use two predominent measurements in allocating aid: population and per capita income. Each formula (there are several hundred different programs, each with a different formula) seeks to balance population and income in some mixture to develop a basis for the allocation of resources but, in doing so, fails to deal fairly with national problems and priorities.

POPULATION

On the face of it, what could be fairer than to distribute federal funds based on population, according to each state the share of federal funds to which its total population entitles it? If a state has 10 percent of America's people, let it get 10 percent of the aid. Because of this seeming equity, population-based aid has become a favorite method of allocating federal assistance. Over 120 federal programs are partially or fully guided by population formulae in their aid allocations.[6]

Unfortunately, population formulae assume that the rich and the poor should be aided equally. In fact, the poor absorb vastly more in the way of services than the wealthy, and most programs are far more in demand in poor areas than in wealthy ones. It is the height of absurdity to allocate, as the federal government now does, social services aid based on population. All communities do not need equally foster care, day care, job training, family counseling, and the like. To pretend that they do have equal needs is to indulge in a mythology uniquely harmful to the American city.

Between 1969 and 1974, the northeastern American city lost population, and those who remained in the city were more likely to be poor. Thus, under population-based aid, cities lost money even as their need for federal aid increased. It is interesting to note that federal spending formulae were adopted linking aid to population at precisely the time during which northeastern cities found their population on the decline, some by precipitous amounts:

POPULATION DECREASES IN NORTHEASTERN CITIES, 1970-73[7]

City	*% Pop. Decline*
St. Louis*	14.2
Minneapolis	12.0
Cleveland	9.6
Detroit	8.4
Pittsburgh	7.8
Chicago	5.8
Philadelphia	4.5
New York	4.1

**1970-74 data for St. Louis.*

Those who remained in cities became poorer than ever during this same period. Between 1969 and 1973, median real income for American major center cities dropped by 1.3 percent while median real income for center city blacks dropped by 6 percent. In New York City, real black income dropped by almost 11 percent over the four years.[8] Cities had fewer people and therefore got less aid, but those who remained were poorer and needed the aid more. Clearly, population-based formulae made it very hard for cities that took their social problems seriously.

But the Ohio experience indicates a second severe problem with the equity of population-based formulae: Simply because a state has enough people to entitle it to federal aid does not mean that it renders services to them. While the poor in the United States are spread throughout the fifty states, it is only in a few places that local governments care enough about their social needs to meet them. The bulk of the nation is incredibly unresponsive to these basic human needs. To allocate funds based on *need* is to ignore the question of whether the need is being met—that is, whether the state is working on programs designed to deal with the social problems. An index of the degree to which social problems are met in certain areas far more than in other parts of the nation is provided by the distribution of welfare recipients. Although the need for welfare is pervasive throughout all the nation's states and cities, eight counties, with 11.4 percent of the nation's population, provide 42.2 percent of the welfare checks in the nation. Presumably the poor in other states and counties are left to fend for themselves.

WELFARE RECIPIENTS COMPARED WITH NATIONAL POPULATION[9]

Area	*% of National Pop.*	*% of National Welfare Recipients*
Cook County (Chicago)	2.6	10.2
New York City	3.6	15.5
Suffolk County (Boston)	1.3	1.9
Wayne County (Detroit)	1.2	5.3
Hennepin County (Minneapolis)	.5	.8
Cuyahoga County (Cleveland)	.8	2.5
Philadelphia	.9	4.8
Milwaukee	.5	1.2
TOTAL	11.4	42.2

One is driven to the conclusion that the rest of the country just doesn't meet the needs of its poor, if these eight urban counties, with only one tenth of the nation's people, have four tenths of the nation's welfare cases. This concentration of social services in urban areas, despite their declining population, indicates more clearly than anything else the inequity of basing federal aid on population criteria.

Yet population continues to be used as a key measurement of aid and spending in a variety of federal programs:[10]

- Work-study (aid to college students)
- Vocational education
- Public library construction
- Assistance to local schools for educationally deprived children
- Education of the handicapped
- Comprehensive employment programs
- Water pollution grants
- Community development and housing
- Social services

These federal programs touch all people in American cities, and their underfunding due to population-based formulae impacts the lives of all urbanites. But protest against population-based formulae has begun to accumulate in recent years. Congressional liberals and representatives of urban areas have insisted in recent years on aid formulae based on per capita incomes and other indices of poverty. Congressman Edward I. Koch of New York told me, for example, that "we are getting away from formulae based strictly on population because they are unfair to cities and are turning more and more to formulae based on income or poverty."

INCOME-BASED FORMULAE

The increasing trend toward income-based allocation formulae raises problems of its own, often unexplored at the congressional level. Any formula based on income or the extent of poverty must be biased in favor of the Sun Belt and the South, since these states have a far lower per capita income than do northern states. This lower per capita income entitles them to a larger share of the federal funds allocated based on income measurements.

If this higher per capita income were reflective of greater real poverty and less real income in the South, it would be quite valid for federal funding programs to use income measurements in determining allocation priorities. Unfortunately, this seemingly lower per capita income in southern states is not truly reflective of greater need, but much more reflective of the lower cost of living in southern and Sun Belt states. Once again, the federal government is failing to recognize cost-of-living differences among regions and the distorting effect these variations have on income data.

Superficially, the Sun Belt appears to have a lower per capita income than the Northeast. On its face the per capita income of the six major Sun Belt cities and their metropolitan areas is 5.9 percent less than in the six largest northeastern cities. But when adjustment is made for cost-of-living differences among the six northern and six southern cities, the northern per capita income is actually 5.3 percent *lower* than the southern income! In *real* terms, as opposed to in terms unadjusted for living costs, the Northeast is actually poorer than the Sun Belt, yet in unadjusted terms it appears to be more wealthy and less in need of federal assistance.

UNADJUSTED AND ADJUSTED* PER CAPITA INCOMES: NORTHEAST AND SUN BELT[11]

Northeast			Sun Belt		
City	*Per Capita Income*		*City*	*Per Capita Income*	
	Unadjusted	*Adjusted*		*Unadjusted*	*Adjusted*
New York	6,209	6,209	Dallas	5,157	6,621
Boston	5,486	5,464	Los Angeles	5,824	6,901
Chicago	6,169	6,940	Houston	5,134	6,650
Philadelphia	5,450	6,137	Atlanta	5,282	6,729
Detroit	6,228	7,187	San Francisco	6,354	7,002
Minneapolis	5,584	6,232	San Diego	5,209	6,224
AVERAGE	5,976	6,436	AVERAGE	5,638	6,778

"Adjusted" income is adjusted for New York City dollars.

Clearly, the indication afforded by per capita income of the relatively greater wealth of the North is an illusion. When cost of living is equalized, there is no question but that northern urban per capita income is below that of southern cities.

The Comprehensive Manpower and Training Act (CETA), the federal public works and job creation program, is pioneering new ground in federal grant formulae. The CETA program is at least partially based on "the ratio that the relative number of adults in families with an annual income below the low income level in the State bears to the total number of such adults for all States." Thus, CETA asks not how many people are poor by any national standard, but how many are poor measured against the "low income level" established by the Bureau of Labor Statistics for each metropolitan area in the nation. Under CETA, a state may have people with lower per capita incomes than another state but yet receive less aid, since its low income level—that is, its living costs for a low-income family—may be determined by the Bureau of Labor Statistics to be lower.[12]

The CETA program should provide a precedent for all income-based funding formulae. Congressional liberals and representatives of northeastern districts should work closely together to bring about an alteration in federal funding formulae to adjust them for cost-of-living differences, thereby permitting northeastern states a fair crack at federal funds.

During 1977, congressional members from the Northeast have begun to work more closely together. Under the influence of such congressional leaders as Congressmen Michael Harrington, House Banking Committee Chairman Henry Reuss, New York Senator Daniel Patrick Moynihan, and Manhattan Congressman Edward I. Koch, members of the House and the Senate from the northeastern and Great Lakes states are beginning to work together to end federal discrimination in grant-in-aid formulae. While their attention to the other aspects of federal discrimination discussed in this book is less than adequate, this congressional group has made substantial progress in modifying federal programs to deal more completely with the needs of the Northeast. Their efforts must continue and increase if the Northeast is to receive a fair share of the $60 billion distributed annually in federal grants to state and local governments.

At the moment, the states of the Northeast receive only $154 per capita in federal grants (exclusive of Medicaid and welfare, neither of which is subject to any limitations on federal matching) while the national average is $170 per year.[13] The fact that the Northeast gets 10 percent less than the national average is especially disturbing in view of the concentration of social and human programs in the Northeast as indicated by the residence of 42 percent of the nation's welfare recipients in eight northeastern counties with 10 percent of the national population. This shortchange not only brings pain and suffering to those in need of federal grant programs but also acts to slow expansion of the public sector at the state and local level in the Northeast and to decrease the stimulus provided by public spending to the region's economy. The less federal money a state receives, the less it can spend and the less it can stimulate its economy without resort to additional taxation. This sap on the economic potential of a state or city to help itself is a key element of the economic stagnation that has gripped the northeastern region.

A FINAL THOUGHT

The picture that emerges from the foregoing analysis is a very different one from that which we have been led, over the years, to accept. We are told that cities are in trouble because of their liberalism, their historic commitment to social and human services, and their high rate of local taxation. We are asked to cut spending on progressive programs and to roll back decades of advance in consumer, environmental, and labor legislation. The very progressive fabric of our cities is attacked as causal of our economic malaise.

But the facts do not bear out this convenient, conservative hypothesis. The deficits of our urban governments are caused more by profiteering in the welfare and Medicaid program by the real estate, nursing home, medical equipment, medical education, social service, and hospital administration industries. When these excessive charges are added to the increased interest costs cities must bear and then viewed against the decrease in property tax revenues brought about by the decline in urban housing, they account for most of the deficit of our cities. The fiscal instability of the American city dates not from a bank decision to avoid the risky bonds of fiscally irresponsible city administrations, but from the banking industry's desire to abandon cities for more profitable forms of investment well before any basis for fiscal insecurity emerged. The decline in urban housing is not the product of liberal social policies or regulation of urban rentals, but rather is due to the refusal of banks to lend mortgages in American cities, which is, in turn, caused in part by the refusal of the federal government to insure such mortgages.

Similarly, the economic decline of the northeastern city stems not from labor unions or environmental groups or consumer organizations, but from the simple realities of economics imposed by federal policies. Cities are condemned to a higher cost of living than is the rest of America by federal energy and food pricing policies that force the Northeast to bear ever increasing costs. By requiring the Northeast to purchase its energy in a costly world market while allowing the rest of the nation to purchase from a controlled domestic market, the costs of electricity, heating oil, and gasoline are greater in northern cities than in other parts of America. Federal regulation of food transportation and dairy pricing policies contribute to an inflation in food costs in the Northeast in excess of that under which the rest of America must labor.

The higher northeastern living costs force northern cities to pay more in federal taxes, get less in federal aid, and receive less valuable federal cash transfer checks. The federal spending bias against the northern city built into the defense program, federal employment patterns, and aid formulae combine with an antiurban bias in income tax regulations to take from cities vastly more in taxes than they receive in federal spending.

This net outflow in funds is the most important element in the decline of the northeastern urban economy. It predestines cities to economic ruin unless they are successful in reversing a trend of decreasing federal spending and increasing federal taxes. This imbalance is the crux of the economic problems of the northeastern city, and it must be addressed before we can anticipate any meaningful progress in bringing the northeastern city back to life and to economic prosperity.

CHAPTER 1

1. In fiscal year 1977, the total allocation for social welfare spending was as follows:

Department of Social Services	$2,974 million
Human Resources Administration	93 million
NYC Health and Hospitals Corporation	796 million
Other Medicaid	379 million
TOTAL	$4,242 million

Of this sum, total payments to AFDC—Aid to Families of Dependent Children—and Home Relief was $1,216 million, of which approximately $400 million went to real property rents. Thus about $800 million of about $4 billion spent, or about twenty cents on the dollar, went in direct payments to welfare recipients.

Data on Department of Social Services is found on page 116, Human Resources Administration on page 228, Health and Hospitals Corporation on page 214, other Medicaid on page 121, and on AFDC and HR payments on page 116 of the Executive Budget of the City of New York for Fiscal Year 1977.

2. City's total Executive Budget for 1977 was $12.5 billion, of which $4.2 billion is one third. According to the New York City Department of Social Services, 813,317 individuals received AFDC payments in July 1977. These individuals were grouped into 252,330 one-parent households. If we presume that the difference between these two figures represents children on AFDC, we can conclude that 560,981 children receive public assistance each year in New York City. According to a report by the Center for New York City Affairs of the New School for Social Research, *New York City's Population—1974,* the total New York City population under the age of seventeen in New York City is 2,235,000, hence the conclusion that one child in four in New York City is on welfare.
3. As summarized in the language of the statute, the Social Security Act authorized money grants to states to assist them in the relief of the "destitute blind and of homeless, crippled, dependent, and delinquent children."
4. U. S. Department of Commerce, Bureau of the Census, *City Government Finances in 1973-74,* and companion works, *County Government Finances* and *State Government Finances.*
5. Ibid.
6. *New York City Expense Budget, 1977.*
7. Among the leading foster-care organizations are Catholic Child Care Society of the Diocese of Brooklyn, Hebrew Children's Home, Henry Street Settlement, Jewish Board of Guardians, Lutheran Community Services, and over ninety other such organizations.
8. Total New York City Expense Budget allocations for foster care increased from $177.8 million in 1974-75 to $199.3 million in 1977-78 according to the New York City Bureau of the Budget.
9. Testimony Before the City Council and Board of Estimate, Executive Budget Hearing, May 16, 1977, New York City, by Joint Action for Children.
10. Meeting on December 20, 1974, with Carol Parry among author, Assemblyman Richard N. Gottfried, and Ms. Parry. Confirmed in telephone conversation with Ms. Parry, August 4, 1977.
11. Blue Heaven Drug Abusers Program, funded by the Addiction Services Agency in 1970 and defunded two years later after a newspaper exposé.
12. Interview with Dr. Rosenthal, August 1974.
13. According to the analysis of the 1975 Census of Housing published by Dr. George Sternlieb and Dr. James W. Hughes, rent-controlled units in New York City dropped from 1,336,000 in 1965 to 642,000 in 1975.
14. According to the 1975 Census of Housing, as interpreted by Sternlieb and Hughes, median rent payments by public assistance families in New York City are $151 per month. According to the Department of Social Services, in 1977, this led to the expenditure of between $400 and $500 million on rental payments for public assistance recipients.
15. 1975 Census of Housing as interpreted by Sternlieb and Hughes.
16. Ibid.
17. *Children's Services: Administration or Assistance,* report by Joint Action for Children, New York City, 1977.
18. Blanche Bernstein, Donald A. Snider, and William Meezan, *Foster Care Needs and Alternatives to Placement,* Center for New York City Affairs, New School for Social Research, November 1975.
19. Interview with Georgia McMurray, June 1977.
20. *New York City Expense Budget, 1977.*
21. U. S. Department of Commerce, Bureau of the Census, *City, County, and State Finances in 1973-74.*

CHAPTER 2

1. Community Services Administration, *Federal Outlays in Summary,* December 1975.
2. Ibid. and Department of Commerce, Bureau of the Census reports of *State, County, and City Government Finances in 1974-75.*

3. Special Senate Committee on the Aging, *Medicaid Mills in 1976,* USGPO Y4 AG4 M46-6, August 1976.
4. 1977 State of the State message of Governor Hugh L. Carey to the New York State Legislature.
5. Interview with Richard Dresner, April 6, 1977.
6. *Financing the Cost of Health Care,* Ohio Temporary State Commission on Health Care Costs, 1973.
7. Interview with James Posner, August 4, 1977. As Mr. Posner indicates, there exist several programs for governmental review of medical industry decisions to acquire new equipment. The problem with these review efforts is that they have been notably ineffective in containing equipment acquisition and bed expansion decisions. Hospitals that do expand are able to depreciate their equipment, despite the fact that it is paid for largely through public reimbursement, and then invest the depreciation in new equipment with virtually no public review.
8. *Hospital Statistics,* 1975 edition, 1974 data, from the American Hospital Association Annual Survey.
9. Ibid.
10. Ibid.
11. Jack Newfield, "Is This the Meanest Man in New York?" *Village Voice,* December 23, 1974.
12. *Home Health Care,* a report by the New York City Health Services Administration, Irving Levison, Project Director, 1973.
13. Ibid.
14. Special Senate Subcommittee on Aging, *Medicaid Mills in 1976.*
15. Ibid.
16. Ibid.

CHAPTER 3

1. Data on state and local bond sales from *Prospects for the Credit Markets in 1977,* Salomon Brothers, p. 26.
2. Ibid.
3. Ibid., p. 34.
4. Ibid., p. 26.
5. Ibid., p. 34.
6. Ibid., pp. 34, 27.
7. Ibid., p. 26.
8. *New York City Expense Budget, 1977* indicates total interest on funded debt of $515 million and on temporary debt of $202 million, totaling $717 million. When this sum is added to the over $200 million in debt service of the Municipal Assistance Corporation, it exceeds the $800 million of public assistance payments exclusive of rent payments to owners of real property renting to welfare tenants.
9. *Prospects for the Credit Markets in 1977,* p. 26.
10. Ibid.
11. Ibid.
12. Interview with New York State Superintendent of Insurance, May 1977.
13. Interview with New Jersey Superintendent of Insurance, June 13, 1977.

CHAPTER 4

1. Citizens Budget Commission, *Pocket Summary of City Finances,* 1965-75.
2. *1975 Census of Housing,* analysis by Dr. George Sternlieb and Dr. James W. Hughes.
3. Ibid.
4. U. S. Department of Commerce, Bureau of the Census, *City Government Finances in 1973-74.*
5. *Bank on Brooklyn,* study by the New York Public Interest Research Group, 1977.

6. Study of the New York State Banking Department revealed that in 1977, the New York State savings banks invested only 35 percent of their new annual financial commitments in New York State mortgages.
7. New York University Real Estate Institute, *Saving New York's Neighborhoods.*
8. Community Services Administration, *Federal Outlays in Summary,* December 1975.
9. Citizens Budget Commission, *Pocket Summary of City Finances,* 1965-75.
10. Ibid.
11. Ibid.
12. U. S. Department of Commerce, Bureau of the Census, *Construction Reports,* Housing Authorized by Building Permits and Public Contracts, 1975.
13. U. S. Department of Labor, Bureau of Labor Statistics, *Autumn 1976 Urban Family Budgets and Comparative Indexes for Selected Urban Areas.*

CHAPTER 5

1. Petroleum Industry Research Foundation, Inc., *Petroleum Imports in 1976.*
2. Federal Energy Administration, Office of Price Regulation.
3. Ibid.
4. U. S. Department of Labor, Bureau of Labor Statistics, *Some Facts Relevant to the Current Economic Scene in New York,* December 5, 1975.
5. New York State Public Service Commission, *Special Analysis of Why Consolidated Edison Costs Exceed Those of Other Utilities,* 1976.
6. Federal Energy Administration, *Per Capita Energy Utilization.*
7. U. S. Department of Commerce, *Balance of Trade Data for 1975.*
8. Ibid.
9. Ibid.

CHAPTER 6

1. U. S. Department of Labor, Bureau of Labor Statistics, *Autumn 1976 Urban Family Budgets and Comparative Indexes for Selected Urban Areas.*
2. U. S. Department of Labor, *Estimated Retail Food Prices By Cities,* 1965-77.
3. Nicholas A. Glaskowsky, Jr., Brian F. O'Neil, and Donald R. Hudson, *Motor Carrier Regulation: A Review and Evaluation of Three Major Current Regulatory Issues Relating to the Interstate Common Carrier Trucking Industry,* ATA Foundation, Washington, D.C., 1976.
4. Federal Highway Administration, *Survey of Interstate Trucking,* 1976.
5. Edward Miller, "Effects of Regulation on Truck Utilization," *Transportation Journal,* Fall 1976. The ICC ruled in the case of Ralph A. Veon, Contract Carrier Application, that "the commission has no duty to foster the growth of private carriage and thus, in effect, preside over the liquidation of carriers subject to its regulation."
6. U. S. Department of Agriculture, *Milk Marketing Order Price Levels,* June 1976.

CHAPTER 7

1. Community Services Administration, *Federal Outlays in Summary,* December 1975.
2. Ibid. and Community Services Administration, *Federal Outlays in New York State,* December 1975.
3. Jack Newfield and Paul DeBrul, *The Abuse of Power* (New York: Viking Press, 1977).
4. Joel Havemann, Neal R. Pierce, and Rochelle L. Stanfield, "Federal Spending: The North's Loss Is the Sunbelt's Gain," *National Journal,* June 26, 1976.
5. *Federal Outlays in Summary* and *Annual Report of the Internal Revenue Service, 1975.* This data does not include expenditures attributed to the

states but really having nothing to do with actual aid or spending they receive. These include: interest on the federal debt which is just passed through federal reserve bank offices in each state and goes throughout the nation, foreign aid payments, support for international organizations, Tennessee Valley Authority bonds, Public Law 480 purchases.

6. Total personal income for the fifteen northeastern states is about $600 billion, of which the net "outflow" of $44 billion is about 6.5 percent.
7. Sources for this calculation are Community Services Administration, *Federal Outlays in Georgia, Texas, and New York;* U. S. Department of Commerce, *City Government Finances in 1973-74;* U. S. Department of Commerce, *County Government Finances in 1973-74;* U. S. Department of Commerce, *State Government Finances in 1973-74; Annual Report of the Internal Revenue Service, 1976.*
8. According to *Special Analyses, Budget of the United States Government, 1977,* Executive Office of the President, $61 billion is spent on grants in aid to states or localities of a total federal budget of $404.5 billion.

CHAPTER 8

1. U. S. Department of Labor, Bureau of Labor Statistics, *Some Facts Relevant to the Current Economic Scene in New York,* December 5, 1975.
2. U. S. Department of Labor, Bureau of Labor Statistics, *Autumn 1976 Urban Family Budgets and Comparative Indexes for Selected Urban Areas.*
3. Ibid.
4. U. S. Department of Commerce, Bureau of the Census, *State, City, and County Finances in 1974-75.*
5. The Tax Foundation, Inc., June 1976.
6. This calculation is derived from Bureau of Labor Statistics cost-of-living data and Bureau of the Census population data.
7. *Autumn 1976 Urban Family Budgets.*
8. This calculation is derived from Bureau of Labor Statistics cost-of-living data as applied to tax collections as reported by the Internal Revenue Service for 1975. It presupposes a complete indexing system in which all currency values would be equalized in real dollar terms.
9. *Special Analyses, Budget of the United States Government, Fiscal Year, 1977,* Analysis F, Tax Expenditures, pp. 127-28.
10. Ibid., p. 128.
11. Ibid., p. 134.
12. This calculation is based on a total rent roll payment in New York City of approximately $4 billion in tax deductions which could be afforded were tax interest and mortgage interest deductible. According to the 1975 Census of Housing the average rent-income ratio in New York is 25 percent. Thus, taxes and interest account for 45 percent of rent or between 10 percent and 12 percent of income.
13. According to New York State Department of Motor Vehicles, of 8.2 million vehicles licensed in New York State, 1.7 million are in New York City.
14. *Special Analyses,* pp. 132-33.
15. U. S. Department of Labor, Bureau of Labor Statistics.
16. The Tax Reduction and Simplification Act, Public Law 95-30.
17. *Special Analyses,* Analysis F.

CHAPTER 9

1. *Special Analyses, Budget of the United States Government, 1977,* Analysis H, U. S. Community Development Administration, and *Federal Outlays in Summary,* 1975.
2. *Federal Outlays in Summary.*
3. *1970 Census of the Population,* Volume I, Characteristics of the Population, Part A, Number of Inhabitants, p. viii. U. S. Civil Service Commission,

Annual Report of Federal Civilian Employment by Geographic Area, 8th ed., December 31, 1973.
4. Computed by equalizing ratios in previous table.

CHAPTER 10

1. Community Development Administration, *Federal Outlays in Texas,* 1975.
2. Community Development Administration, *Federal Outlays in Summary* 1975.
3. Ibid.
4. Telephone conversation with Senator Moynihan in January 1976.
5. U. S. Department of Defense, *Federal Military Installations,* January 1976.

CHAPTER 11

1. Letter from Atlantic Richfield Company.
2. Interview with Richard Shinn, President, Metropolitan Life Insurance Company, July 1977.
3. *Special Analyses Budget of the United States Government, 1977,* Special Analysis A.
4. Ibid.
5. U. S. Department of Labor, Bureau of Labor Statistics, *Living Costs for a Retired Couple, 1975.*
6. Community Development Administration, *Federal Outlays in Summary, 1975.*
7. Bureau of Labor Statistics autumn 1976 cost-of-living data computed in a weighted average.
8. Social Security Administration Tax Collection Data, 1973.
9. Community Development Administration, *Federal Outlays in Summary,* 1975.
10. U. S. Department of Labor, Bureau of Labor Statistics, *1975 Urban Living Costs for a Lower Income Family.*
11. Center for New York City Affairs, New School for Social Research, *New York City's Population—1974.*

CHAPTER 12

1. Library of Congress, Congressional Research Service, *Federal Formula Grant-in-Aid Programs that Use Population as a Factor in Allocating Funds,* 1975.
2. *Special Analyses, Budget of the United States Government, 1977,* Special Analysis O.
3. Citizens Budget Commission, *Pocket Summary of City Finances,* 1965-75.
4. Harrison J. Goldin, "Funds City," *The New York Times,* April 2, 1975.
5. *Pocket Summary of City Finances.*
6. *Federal Formula Grant-in-Aid Programs.*
7. Center for New York City Affairs, New School for Social Research, *New York City's Population—1974.*
8. Ibid.
9. Telephone conversations with Departments of Social Services in each county.
10. *Federal Formula Grant-in-Aid Programs.*
11. Per capita incomes as reported by Bureau of Labor Statistics adjusted for cost-of-living levels of intermediate-income families as reported by the bureau for 1975. Averages are weighted by population.
12. *Federal Formula Grant-in-Aid Programs.*
13. *Special Analysis, Budget of the United States,* Analysis O, adjusted for removal of Medicaid and public assistance expenditures as obtained from Community Development Administration, *Federal Outlays in Summary.*

Abrams, Robert, 6
Abuse of Power, The (Newfield and DeBrul), 112
Addabbo, Joseph, 151
Agnew, Spiro, 4, 116
Agriculture Committee (House of Representatives), 169
American Medical Association, 35
Armed Services Committees (House of Representatives and Senate), 150-151, 152
Atlantic Richfield Company, 162

Banks, 12, 51-66
Beame, Abraham D., 176
Beck, Dave, 105
Bellevue Hospital, 40-41
Bergman, Bernard, 43-44
Bowery Savings Bank, 67
Brooklyn Jewish Hospital, 43
Buckley, James L., 4-5, 8
Budd Corporation, 132-133
Budget Committee (Congressional), 115
Bureau of Children's Services (N.Y.C.), 26
Bureau of Labor Statistics, 100, 124-125, 127-128, 142, 165, 166, 170-171, 183

Carey, Hugh L., 8, 9, 37, 63, 64
Carr, Bob 151
Carter, Jimmy, 3, 29, 86, 89, 132, 134-135, 145

Casualty insurance companies, 61-62, 64-65
Celeste, Richard, 110-111, 175-176
"Charitable Institutions Budget," 21
Citibank, 51
Citizens Budget Commission, 6, 68
Coal, 88-89, 91, 95
Community Services Society, 1
Comprehensive Manpower and Training Act (CETA), 183
Consumer Price Index, 124
Cost of living, 82-83, 99-108, 123-129, 161-173
Crown Heights (Brooklyn), 74

Day-care program (N.Y.C.), 28-29
De Brul, Paul, 112
Deductions, tax, 129-139
Defense spending, distribution of, 147-159
Department of Agriculture (U.S.), 106-108
Department of Commerce (U.S.), 109-110, 124
Department of Health, Education, and Welfare (U.S.), 35
Department of Housing and Urban Development (U.S.), 81
Department of Social Services (N.Y.C.), 19, 30
Downey, Tom, 151
Dresner, Richard, 37-38
Drug addiction programs, 22-23
Dyson, John, 8-9

Emergency Financial Control Board, 58
Energy costs compared, 3, 86-97
Energy crisis, 86
Energy policy, 13, 86-97

Federal funds, distribution of
by income-based formulae, 181-184
by population, 178-181
Federal Highway Administration, 104
Federal Housing Administration (FHA), 75-80
Federal jobs, distribution of, 142-145
Federal Power Commission, 89
First National City Bank of New York—Citibank, 51
Food prices, 99-108
Food Stamp Program, 168-171
Ford, Gerald, 3, 4, 11, 58, 79, 80, 81, 116, 151, 153, 178
Foster care for children, 20-21, 26-28
Friedman, Milton, 129
Fuel costs, 3, 69, 70-71, 86-97

Gates, Gary Paul, 4
General Electric, 9
Gibson, Kenneth A., 3
Goldin, Harrison J., 6, 40, 178
Gorman, Aileen, 101, 107
Great Society, 17
Grey, Ed, 132

Harrington, Michael, 183
Harris, Louis, 74
Health Department (N.Y.C.), 28
Health Services Administration (N.Y.C.), 39, 44-45
Hess, John, 44
Hicks, Louise Day, 5, 8
Hoffa, Jimmy, 105, 106
Hoover, Herbert, 127
House Subcommittee on Domestic Marketing, Consumer Relations, and Nutrition, 169
Housing, 71-83
Housing and Community Development Act (1974), 80-81
Housing welfare, 23-26

Income-based formulae, 181-184
Income tax system, 12-13, 105-139
Indexing, 128-129, 135, 171-172
Institute for the Study of the City, 153
International Union of Electrical Workers, 154
Interstate Commerce Act (1887), 102
Interstate Commerce Commission (ICC), 102-105, 107
Investment tax credit, 132-134

Johnson, Lyndon, 3, 17, 22, 29, 34, 35, 117
Joint Action for Children, 20, 26, 27, 29

Kennedy, John F., 35, 111
Kennedy (Lt. Joseph P., Jr.) Home, 26, 27
Keynes, John Maynard, 111, 113

Koch, Edward I., 45, 181, 183
Koppell, Oliver, 9-10

La Guardia, Fiorello, 110
Larsen, John W., 67, 68-69
Lehman, Herbert, 110
Lekachman, Robert, 129
Lindsay, John, 5, 110
Lockheed Corporation, 156

McDonnell-Douglas Corporation, 158
McMurray, Georgia, 28, 29
Medicaid, 16, 17, 19, 33-50
Medicaid mills, 47-50
Metropolitan Life Insurance Corporation, 162
Metzenbaum, Howard, 11
Military installations, distribution of, 156-157
Milk prices, 106-107
Mitchell, John, 80
Mortgage lenders, 12, 67-69, 70-71, 73-78
Moss, Frank, 47-49, 50
Moynihan, Daniel Patrick, 4-5, 154, 183
Municipal Assistance Corporation, 58
Municipal unions, 61-62, 64

Nader, Ralph, 10
National Center for Telephone Research, 37
National Conference of Mayors, 145
National Consumers' Congress, 101
National Housing Act (1934), 75
National Journal, 112, 115
Natural gas, 89-91, 95
New School for Social Research, 28
New York Affairs, 153
New York City
  banks, importance of to, 58-60
  budget, 21
  Bureau of Children's Services, 26
  day-care program, 28-29
  default crisis, 58-59
  Department of Social Services, 30
  federal jobs, loss of, 142
  fiscal crisis, 1, 7-8
  Health Department, 28
  Health Services Administration, 44-45
  housing welfare, 23-26
  layoffs, 1, 8, 9, 110
  municipal unions, 61-62, 64
  social services to children, 26-30
  unemployment, 2-3, 8
New York *Daily News* (newspaper), 3-4
New York Public Interest Research Group, 73, 77
New York State Department of Banking, 73
New York Times, The (newspaper), 8, 11, 44
New York University Real Estate Institute, 23, 73-74
New York University School of Medicine, 40-41, 42
Newfield, Jack, 44-112
Nixon, Richard M., 3, 4, 9, 10, 11, 76, 78, 79, 80, 116, 153, 177, 178
Nursing homes, 37-38, 43-47

O'Dwyer, Paul, 6
Office of Management and Budget, 115
Oil, 86-89, 91, 95
OPEC, 69, 87, 93-95
Op-Ed page (*The New York Times*), 4-5

Palace Guard, The (Rather and Gates), 4
Parry, Carol, 21
Pentagon, 13, 147-159
Phoenix House, 22
Ping-Ponging, 34, 49
Population-based formulae, 178-181
Posner, James, 38-39
Power Shift, The (Sale), 11
Pratt Institute, 23, 24
Procaccino, Mario, 5, 8
Public Affairs Research Organization, 6
"Public Assistance" ("PA"), 23-24

Rangel, Charles, 129
Rather, Dan, 4
Rattner, Carol, 43-44
Reagan, Ronald, 143
Redlining, 70, 77-78
Reid, Ogden, 9
Rents, 69-70
Reuss, Henry, 183
Rhodes, James, 175-176
Richmond, Fred W., 169

Rizzo, Frank, 5, 6, 8
Rockefeller, Nelson, 18
Roosevelt Franklin D., 16, 110, 127, 168
Rosenthal, Mitchell, 22, 23
Ross, Donald, 77

Sale, Kirkpatrick, 11
Salmon, Thomas P., 11, 90-91
Samuels, Howard J., 6
San Antonio, Texas, 147-148
Savings banks, 61-64, 67-69, 74-75
Schroeder, Pat, 151
Sheerin, James, 65
Simon, William, 50
Slattery, Joan, 33-34
Smith, Alfred E., 110
"Social Issue," 4
Social Security Act of 1935, 16-17
Social Security system, 13, 164-168
Social services, federal grants for, 175-178
State Board of Social Welfare (New York State), 27-28
Steingut, Stanley, 6, 11, 39, 67, 68
Stokes, Carl, 5
Subcommittee on Longer Term Care of the United States Senate Committee on Aging, 47-49
Summary of Federal Outlays in New York State: 1974, 109
Sutton, Percy E., 6, 11, 15-16, 113, 123-124, 128

Tax expenditures, 136-139
Tax revenues to cities, 110-117
Taxes, real property, 69, 72-73
Teamsters Union, 105
Title XX (Social Security Act of 1975), 175-176
Truman, Harry S, 35

United Auto Workers, 132
University of California, 150

Village Voice, The (newspaper), 11, 44

Wagner, Robert, 110
Wallace, George, 76
War on Poverty, 22-23
Ways and Means Committee (House of Representatives), 129
Weiss, Theodore S., 152
Welfare, 12, 15-31
White, Kevin, 5
Willoughby Nursing Home, 43-44

Youthful Drug Abusers Program, 22